D1630369

BEST OF **Good Housekeeping**
30-Minute
Recipes

BEST OF **Good Housekeeping**
30-Minute Recipes

EBURY PRESS
LONDON

First published in 1994

This paperback edition published in 1997

1 3 5 7 9 10 8 6 4 2

Copyright © Random House UK Ltd and The National Magazine Company Ltd 1994

First published in the United Kingdom in 1994
by Ebury Press, Random House, 20 Vauxhall Bridge Road,
London SW1V 2SA

Random House Australia (Pty) Limited
20 Alfred Street, Milsons Point, Sydney
New South Wales 2061, Australia

Random House New Zealand Limited
18 Poland Road, Glenfield
Auckland 10, New Zealand

Random House South Africa (Pty) Limited
Endulini, 5a Jubilee Road, Parktown 2193, South Africa

Random House UK Limited Reg. No. 954009

A CIP catalogue record for this book is available from the British Library.

Editor: Helen Southall
Design: Christine Wood

ISBN 0 09 185313 3 (paperback)
ISBN 0 09 178387 9 (hardback)

Typeset by Textype Typesetters, Cambridge
Printed in Singapore by
Tien Wah Press

CONTENTS

SPEEDY SOUPS AND STARTERS

WHITE BEAN SOUP

PREPARATION TIME: 10 minutes
COOKING TIME: 15 minutes

Pecorino is a delicious, strong-flavoured Italian cheese.

SERVES 4

15 ml (1 tbsp) oil
125 g (4 oz) onion, skinned and finely chopped
1 garlic clove, skinned and crushed
10 ml (2 level tsp) chopped fresh rosemary or
2.5 ml (½ level tsp) dried
425 g (15 oz) can haricot beans, drained
and rinsed
1.1 litres (2 pints) vegetable stock
salt and pepper
125 g (4 oz) Pecorino or Lancashire cheese,
very thinly sliced
toasted wholemeal croûtons and sprigs of fresh
rosemary, to garnish

1 Heat the oil in a large saucepan and sauté
the onion with the garlic and rosemary for 1–2
minutes. Add the beans, stock and salt and pepper to taste. Bring to the boil, then reduce the
heat, cover and simmer for 10 minutes.
2 Purée half the soup mixture in a blender or
food processor and return to the pan. Bring
back to the boil, stirring all the time. Adjust the
seasoning.

3 Serve the soup poured over thin slices of
Pecorino or Lancashire cheese, and sprinkled
with croûtons. Garnish each bowl with a sprig
of rosemary.

NOT SUITABLE FOR FREEZING

255 Calories per serving

HOT AND SOUR PRAWN SOUP

PREPARATION TIME: 5 minutes
COOKING TIME: 20 minutes

SERVES 4

15 ml (1 tbsp) oil
125 g (4 oz) onion, skinned and chopped
1 small green chilli, deseeded and finely chopped
2.5 cm (1 inch) piece of fresh root ginger,
peeled and chopped
50 g (2 oz) small oyster mushrooms
1.1 litres (2 pints) chicken stock
1 lemon grass stalk
15 ml (1 tbsp) white wine vinegar
350 g (12 oz) large cooked peeled prawns,
roughly chopped

1 bunch of watercress, chopped
salt and pepper

Hot and Sour Prawn Soup

1 Heat the oil in a large saucepan and fry the onion, chilli and ginger for 4–5 minutes. Add the mushrooms and continue to fry for 1–2 minutes.

2 Stir in the chicken stock, lemon grass and vinegar. Bring to the boil, then reduce the heat, cover and simmer for 10–12 minutes.

3 Add the prawns and watercress, and simmer for a further 2 minutes. Remove the lemon grass, adjust the seasoning and serve.

NOT SUITABLE FOR FREEZING

140 Calories per serving

VARIATION

Replace the watercress with 60 ml (4 level tbsp) chopped fresh coriander.

CHINESE-STYLE HOT AND SOUR SOUP

PREPARATION TIME: 10 minutes

COOKING TIME: 20 minutes

SERVES 4

225 g (8 oz) button mushrooms, wiped and thinly sliced

100 ml (4 fl oz) medium-dry sherry

75 ml (5 tbsp) soy sauce

30 ml (2 level tbsp) chopped fresh coriander

1.1 litres (2 pints) water

225 g (8 oz) cooked chicken meat, shredded

125 g (4 oz) spring onions, trimmed and shredded

125 g (4 oz) baby sweetcorn, halved

75 ml (5 tbsp) white wine vinegar

freshly ground black pepper

fresh coriander, to garnish

1 Place the mushrooms in a large saucepan with the sherry, soy sauce, coriander and water. Bring to the boil, then reduce the heat and simmer, uncovered, for about 15 minutes.

2 Stir the chicken, spring onions and sweetcorn into the mushroom mixture with the wine vinegar. Add pepper to taste and simmer for a further 5 minutes. Serve hot, garnished with fresh coriander leaves.

NOT SUITABLE FOR FREEZING

150 Calories per serving

LENTIL SOUP

PREPARATION TIME: 10 minutes

COOKING TIME: 20 minutes

SERVES 2

10 ml (2 tsp) vegetable oil

1 potato, about 125 g (4 oz), peeled and roughly chopped

1 onion, about 125 g (4 oz), skinned and roughly chopped

1 carrot, about 50 g (2 oz), peeled and roughly chopped

2 celery sticks, trimmed and roughly chopped

50 g (2 oz) lean smoked back bacon, derinded and chopped

1 garlic clove, skinned and crushed

50 g (2 oz) red lentils

300 ml (½ pint) semi-skimmed milk

300 ml (½ pint) chicken stock

salt and pepper

1 tomato, roughly chopped

1 Heat the oil in a large saucepan, add the vegetables, bacon and garlic, and sauté for 5–10 minutes.

2 Rinse the lentils in cold water, add to the pan and cook for a further 5 minutes. Add the milk, stock and salt and pepper to taste, and bring to the boil. Reduce the heat and simmer for 15–20 minutes or until tender, stirring occasionally.

3 Stir in the roughly chopped tomato and cook for a further 5 minutes. Serve piping hot.

SUITABLE FOR FREEZING

270 Calories per serving

SPICY BEAN AND COURGETTE SOUP

PREPARATION TIME: 10 minutes
COOKING TIME: 20 minutes

SERVES 4

30 ml (2 tbsp) olive oil
175 g (6 oz) onions, skinned and finely chopped
2 garlic cloves, skinned and crushed
10 ml (2 level tsp) ground coriander
15 ml (1 level tbsp) paprika
5 ml (1 level tsp) mild curry powder
450 g (1 lb) courgettes, halved lengthways and sliced
225 g (8 oz) potatoes, peeled and diced
400 g (14 oz) can red kidney beans, drained and rinsed
425 g (15 oz) can flageolet beans, drained and rinsed
1.4 litres (2½ pints) vegetable stock
salt and pepper
crusty bread, to serve

1 Heat the oil in a saucepan and sauté the onions and garlic for 2 minutes. Add the spices and cook, stirring, for 1 minute. Mix in the courgettes and potatoes, and cook for 1–2 minutes.

2 Add the remaining ingredients, cover and simmer for 15 minutes, stirring occasionally, or until the potatoes are tender. Adjust the seasoning before serving with crusty bread.

NOT SUITABLE FOR FREEZING

290 Calories per serving

CHEESY VEGETABLE SOUP

PREPARATION TIME: 10 minutes
COOKING TIME: 20 minutes

SERVES 3–4

30 ml (2 tbsp) oil
50 g (2 oz) onion, skinned and finely chopped
225 g (8 oz) old potatoes, peeled and roughly diced
125 g (4 oz) courgettes, halved lengthways and thinly sliced
125 g (4 oz) sweetcorn kernels
30 ml (2 level tbsp) plain flour
600 ml (1 pint) chicken stock
150 ml (¼ pint) milk
large pinch of cayenne pepper (optional)
salt and pepper
150 g (5 oz) mature Cheddar cheese, grated

1 Heat the oil in a saucepan and fry the onion for 5 minutes or until soft.

2 Add the potato and courgette to the saucepan with the sweetcorn and sauté until coated in oil. Stir in the flour and cook gently for 1–2 minutes before adding the stock with the milk, cayenne pepper, if using, and salt and pepper to taste.

3 Bring to the boil, then reduce the heat, cover and simmer gently for 10–12 minutes or until the vegetables are tender. Stir in the cheese and adjust the seasoning before serving.

NOT SUITABLE FOR FREEZING

475 Calories per serving for 3
360 Calories per serving for 4

TOMATO SOUP WITH BACON

PREPARATION TIME: 5 minutes
COOKING TIME: 20 minutes

SERVES 2–3

30 ml (2 tbsp) oil
125 g (4 oz) onion, skinned and thinly sliced
75 g (3 oz) lean bacon, derinded and roughly chopped
400 g (14 oz) can butter beans, drained and rinsed
300 ml (½ pint) tomato juice
300 ml (½ pint) beef stock
5 ml (1 level tsp) tomato purée
1 bay leaf
salt and pepper

1 Heat the oil in a medium-sized saucepan and sauté the onion for 2–3 minutes or until beginning to soften. Add the bacon and cook for a further 2–3 minutes or until it begins to brown, stirring frequently.
2 Add the beans to the saucepan with the remaining ingredients.
3 Bring to the boil, then reduce the heat, cover and simmer for about 15 minutes. Remove the bay leaf and adjust the seasoning before serving the soup.

SUITABLE FOR FREEZING

450 Calories per serving for 2
300 Calories per serving for 3

LEMON AND PARSLEY SOUP

PREPARATION TIME: 2 minutes
COOKING TIME: 15 minutes

This soup is best made with homemade chicken stock.

SERVES 3

6 large spring onions
25 g (1 oz) butter
15 ml (1 level tbsp) plain flour
900 ml (1½ pints) well-flavoured chicken stock
45 ml (3 tbsp) lemon juice
2 egg yolks
75 ml (5 tbsp) single cream
45 ml (3 level tbsp) chopped fresh parsley, preferably flat-leaf
salt and pepper

1 Finely slice the onions, reserving some of the green tops for garnish. Melt the butter in a saucepan and sauté the onions for about 5 minutes or until soft.
2 Stir in the flour, followed by the stock and lemon juice. Bring to the boil, then reduce the heat and simmer for 10 minutes. Remove from the heat and strain.
3 Beat the egg yolks with the cream and add the strained stock. Return everything to the pan with the parsley, then add salt and pepper to taste. Bring to serving temperature without boiling, and serve garnished with finely snipped onion tops.

NOT SUITABLE FOR FREEZING

195 Calories per serving

CARROT AND ORANGE SOUP

PREPARATION TIME: 10 minutes
COOKING TIME: 15 minutes

SERVES 2

350 g (12 oz) carrots, peeled and thinly sliced
50 g (2 oz) onion, skinned and thinly sliced
a few sprigs of fresh mint
600 ml (1 pint) water
1 vegetable stock cube
50 ml (2 fl oz) unsweetened orange juice
50 g (2 oz) mushrooms, wiped and sliced
salt and pepper
croûtons, to garnish

1 Put the carrot and onion in a saucepan with the mint, water and stock cube. Bring to the boil, then reduce the heat, cover and simmer for about 15 minutes or until the vegetables are tender.
2 Purée the soup in a blender or food processor, then return it to the pan and add the orange juice and mushrooms. Add salt and pepper to taste, heat through gently, then serve sprinkled with croûtons.

NOT SUITABLE FOR FREEZING

90 Calories per serving

VARIATION

Serve sprinkled with a few lightly toasted chopped almonds.

STUFFED BAKED MUSHROOMS

PREPARATION TIME: 10 minutes
COOKING TIME: 10 minutes

SERVES 4

8 large flat mushrooms
25 g (1 oz) butter
125 g (4 oz) onions, skinned and finely chopped
1 garlic clove, skinned and crushed
50 g (2 oz) cup mushrooms, wiped and chopped
30 ml (2 level tbsp) chopped fresh parsley
400 g (14 oz) can chick peas, drained and chopped
50 g (2 oz) Gouda cheese, grated
salt and pepper
15 ml (1 tbsp) lemon juice
50 g (2 oz) Parmesan cheese, freshly grated
4 large slices of wholemeal bread, toasted
paprika and sprigs of fresh parsley, to garnish

1 Roughly chop the flat mushroom stalks.
2 Melt the butter in a large sauté pan, add the onions and garlic and cook until beginning to soften. Stir in all the chopped mushrooms and cook over a high heat, stirring continuously, until well reduced. Mix in the parsley, chick peas and Gouda. Add salt and pepper to taste.
3 Lightly oil a shallow ovenproof dish. Arrange the flat mushrooms in the dish in a single layer and spoon in the stuffing. Drizzle over the lemon juice and sprinkle over the Parmesan.
4 Bake in the oven at 200°C (400°F) mark 6 for 10 minutes. Serve on slices of toast, dusted with paprika and garnished with parsley.

NOT SUITABLE FOR FREEZING

435 Calories per serving

CHEESY SPINACH FLAN

PREPARATION TIME: 5–10 minutes
COOKING TIME: 25 minutes

For speed of preparation, this tasty cheese flan makes use of convenience foods such as packets of ready-grated cheese and frozen spinach and pastry, leaving only the courgettes to be grated and the flan case to be baked. Although the finished flan is not suitable for freezing, the baked, unfilled pastry case can be wrapped and stored in the refrigerator for a few days. The flan can then be put together and finished off under the grill in a matter of 10 minutes or so.

SERVES 4

370 g (13 oz) shortcrust pastry, thawed if frozen
1 egg, beaten
250 g (8.82 oz) packet grated Cheddar cheese
450 g (1 lb) pack frozen creamed spinach
225 g (8 oz) courgettes, coarsely grated
large pinch of freshly grated nutmeg
salt and pepper
25 g (1 oz) flaked almonds

1 Roll out the pastry thinly and use to line a 20.5–23 cm (8–9 inch) metal flan ring on a baking sheet. Prick the base with a fork and line with greaseproof paper and baking beans. Reroll the remaining pastry and stamp out as many 5 cm (2 inch) rounds as possible. Place alongside the flan ring on the baking sheet. Brush the rounds with beaten egg and sprinkle with a little of the grated cheese. Bake the flan and rounds in the oven at 200°C (400°F) mark 6 for 20 minutes or until the pastry is cooked through and the rounds bubbling and golden. Cool the rounds on a wire rack.

2 While the pastry is baking, make the filling. Thaw the creamed spinach in a medium-sized saucepan, stirring occasionally. Add the courgettes, nutmeg, half the remaining cheese and salt and pepper to taste. Stir for 2–3 minutes over a high heat to drive off any excess moisture, then spoon into the prepared flan case. Sprinkle with the remaining cheese and the flaked almonds.

3 Place under a hot grill for 3–4 minutes until golden and bubbling. Serve hot or warm with the cheese pastries.

NOT SUITABLE FOR FREEZING

780 Calories per serving

VARIATION

Use packs of frozen creamed leeks instead of the spinach.

CHORIZO, FETA AND AUBERGINE PIZZA

PREPARATION TIME: 10 minutes
COOKING TIME: 20 minutes

Vacuum-packed pizza bases make this a really speedy recipe.

SERVES 6

2 long-life pizza bases, about 22 cm (8½ inches) in diameter
50 ml (2 fl oz) olive oil
450 g (1 lb) tomatoes, sliced
1 small aubergine, about 175 g (6 oz), thinly sliced
150 g (5 oz) chorizo or spicy sausage
125 g (4 oz) feta cheese
15 ml (1 level tbsp) roughly chopped fresh oregano
black pepper
oregano leaves, to garnish

1 Place the pizza bases on baking sheets and brush lightly with olive oil. Arrange the tomato slices on top, making sure they cover the bases right up to the edges. Tuck the aubergine slices in between the tomato slices.
2 Cut the sausage into chunks and scatter over the pizzas. Crumble the feta cheese and sprinkle over the pizzas with the oregano. Season with pepper only, as feta is salty. Drizzle with the remaining olive oil.
3 Bake in the oven at 220°C (425°F) mark 7 for 15–20 minutes. Cut each pizza into three portions and serve immediately, garnished with oregano leaves.

NOT SUITABLE FOR FREEZING

300 Calories per serving

DEVILLED MUSHROOM BAGUETTES

PREPARATION TIME: 5 minutes
COOKING TIME: 10 minutes

SERVES 4

75–125 g (3–4 oz) butter or margarine
175 g (6 oz) onions, skinned and finely chopped
1 garlic clove, skinned and crushed
350 g (12 oz) button mushrooms, wiped and sliced
30 ml (2 tbsp) vinegar, preferably red wine vinegar
5 ml (1 level tsp) mustard powder
a dash of Worcestershire or Tabasco sauce
30 ml (2 tbsp) tomato ketchup
salt and pepper
1 long French loaf (baguette)
30 ml (2 level tbsp) chopped fresh parsley

1 Melt 50 g (2 oz) butter or margarine in a small saucepan. Add the onion and garlic and cook for 3–4 minutes or until beginning to soften.
2 Mix in the mushrooms and stir over a high heat for a further 3–4 minutes. Add the vinegar, mustard, sauce, ketchup, and salt and pepper to taste. Simmer gently for 1–2 minutes.
3 Meanwhile, cut the baguette in half, and then cut each piece in half lengthways to give four long pieces. Toast under the grill, then spread lightly with butter. Spoon the warm mushroom mixture over the pieces of bread, sprinkle with parsley and serve immediately.

NOT SUITABLE FOR FREEZING

335 Calories per serving

GARLIC-CRUSTED RATATOUILLE

PREPARATION TIME: 5 minutes
COOKING TIME: 15 minutes

SERVES 6

390 g (13.7 oz) can ratatouille
200 g (7 oz) can tuna fish in brine, drained and roughly flaked
30 ml (2 tbsp) dry sherry
60 ml (4 level tbsp) chopped fresh parsley
125 g (4 oz) frozen green beans
3 garlic cloves, skinned
175 g (6 oz) tomatoes, chopped
1 small baguette
30 ml (2 tbsp) olive oil

1 Put the ratatouille in a saucepan with the tuna, sherry, parsley and green beans. Crush one of the garlic cloves and add it to the pan. Simmer the mixture for 3–4 minutes or until the beans are tender. Stir in the tomatoes. Bring to the boil and simmer for 2–3 minutes or until the mixture is piping hot.
2 Meanwhile, slice the bread into 1 cm (½ inch) slices. Place on a baking sheet and toast one side under the grill. Crush the remaining garlic and mix it with the olive oil. Turn the bread slices over, drizzle with the oil and toast lightly.
3 Serve the ratatouille mixture topped with the slices of garlic bread.

NOT SUITABLE FOR FREEZING

235 Calories per serving

AVOCADO WITH CHICKEN

PREPARATION TIME: 5 minutes
COOKING TIME: nil

SERVES 4

125 g (4 oz) cooked chicken breast, roughly chopped
1 bunch of spring onions, trimmed and roughly chopped
30 ml (2 level tbsp) mayonnaise
30 ml (2 tbsp) lemon juice
salt and pepper
2 small ripe avocados
grated orange rind and watercress sprigs, to garnish

1 Mix the chicken and spring onions with the mayonnaise, lemon juice and salt and pepper to taste.
2 Halve the avocados and remove the stones. Carefully scoop out the flesh and roughly dice. Stir into the chicken and mayonnaise mixture, then spoon back into the avocado shells.
3 Garnish with orange rind and watercress before serving.

NOT SUITABLE FOR FREEZING

220 Calories per serving

Avocado with Chicken

14

TAGLIATELLE WITH WALNUTS AND CHEESE

PREPARATION TIME: 5 minutes
COOKING TIME: 15–20 minutes

Medium tagliatelle looks best in this recipe, although finer varieties will cook more quickly.

SERVES 4–6

225 g (8 oz) medium or fine tagliatelle
salt and pepper
olive oil
3 eggs
142 g (5 oz) packet full- or low-fat soft cheese
with garlic and herbs
50 g (2 oz) butter or polyunsaturated margarine
50 g (2 oz) walnut pieces, roughly chopped
chopped fresh parsley

1 Cook the tagliatelle in boiling salted water, with a dash of added oil, according to packet instructions or until just tender. Drain.
2 Whisk together the eggs, cheese and salt and pepper to taste.
3 Heat the butter or margarine with 30 ml (2 tbsp) oil in a large saucepan. Add the nuts and brown lightly. Mix in the pasta and cook, stirring, until hot right through.
4 Add the egg mixture and stir over a gentle heat until the eggs are just beginning to set. Stir in parsley to taste and adjust the seasoning before serving.

NOT SUITABLE FOR FREEZING

508 Calories per serving for 4
339 Calories per serving for 6

SMOKED MACKEREL AND WATERCRESS MOUSSE

PREPARATION TIME: 20 minutes
COOKING TIME: nil

For speed, this mousse is quickly chilled in the freezer. If time allows, chill in the refrigerator for an hour.

SERVES 4

1 small bunch of watercress
175 g (6 oz) smoked mackerel fillet, skinned
125 g (4 oz) low-fat soft cheese
60 ml (4 tbsp) low-fat natural yogurt
30 ml (2 tbsp) lemon juice
15 ml (1 level tbsp) creamed horseradish
black pepper
1 egg white
rye bread and lemon wedges, to serve

1 Rinse the watercress in cold water and drain. Discard any coarse stalks, reserve a few sprigs for garnish, and place the remaining watercress in a food processor.
2 Add the mackerel to the processor with the cheese, yogurt, lemon juice, horseradish and plenty of black pepper. Blend until quite smooth.
3 Whisk the egg white until stiff but not dry. Fold in the mackerel mixture and spoon into four ramekin dishes. Cover and freeze for 10–15 minutes only – just long enough for the mixture to firm up slightly.
4 Garnish with watercress sprigs and serve with thin slices of rye bread and wedges of lemon.

NOT SUITABLE FOR FREEZING

135 Calories per serving

MINTED CUCUMBER PÂTÉ WITH FLAGEOLET SALAD

PREPARATION TIME: 10 minutes
COOKING TIME: nil

SERVES 6

two 400 g (14 oz) cans flageolet or cannellini
beans, drained and rinsed
450 g (1 lb) curd cheese
a bunch of fresh mint
grated rind of ½ lemon
50 g (2 oz) natural peanuts, walnuts or hazelnuts
½ cucumber, about 225 g (8 oz)
2.5 ml (½ level tsp) garlic salt
black pepper
45 ml (3 tbsp) French dressing
sprigs of herbs, sliced cucumber and lemon
slices, to garnish
wholemeal toast, to serve

1 Place half the beans in a food processor with the curd cheese, a small handful of mint, the grated lemon rind and the nuts. Blend until almost smooth and transfer to a bowl.
2 Coarsely grate the cucumber into a clean tea-towel and squeeze to remove excess moisture. Beat the cucumber into the cheese mixture with the garlic salt and black pepper to taste.
3 Toss the remaining beans and 45 ml (3 level tbsp) chopped mint with the French dressing. Serve with the pâté. Garnish with herbs, cucumber and lemon. Serve with toast.

NOT SUITABLE FOR FREEZING

340 Calories per serving

CHICORY AND CARROT GRATIN

PREPARATION TIME: 10 minutes
COOKING TIME: 16 minutes

This is good served with warm bread, such as garlic focaccia.

SERVES 4

175 g (6 oz) carrots, peeled and sliced
salt and pepper
4 heads of chicory
142 ml (5 fl oz) carton of soured cream
½ garlic clove, skinned and crushed

1 Cook the carrots in boiling salted water for about 4 minutes or until just tender. Drain. Thickly slice the chicory, discarding the thick core.
2 Mix together all the ingredients and place in a shallow flameproof dish. Season well with salt and plenty of pepper.
3 Place under a moderate grill for 10 minutes, then turn the heat to high for a further 2 minutes or until brown.
4 Serve immediately on its own or with warm bread.

NOT SUITABLE FOR FREEZING

90 Calories per serving

*P*AN-FRIED TOMATOES

PREPARATION TIME: 8 minutes
COOKING TIME: 3 minutes

SERVES 4

100 ml (4 fl oz) olive oil
2 garlic cloves, skinned and sliced lengthways
450 g (1 lb) plum tomatoes, thickly sliced
30 ml (2 level tbsp) capers, drained and rinsed
30 ml (2 level tbsp) chopped fresh parsley
25 g (1 oz) canned anchovies, drained (optional)
rock salt
coarsely ground black pepper
toasted ciabatta bread and fresh goat's cheese,
to serve

1 Heat the olive oil with the garlic in a large frying pan. Add the tomatoes and fry for 1 minute only on each side. Using a slotted spoon, remove to a shallow serving dish.

2 Add all the remaining ingredients to the pan and heat for 1 minute, stirring. Pour over the tomatoes. Serve warm or cold with toasted ciabatta bread and goat's cheese.

NOT SUITABLE FOR FREEZING

240 Calories per serving

Pan-Fried Tomatoes

TROUT FILLETS EN CROÛTE

PREPARATION TIME: 10 minutes
COOKING TIME: 20–25 minutes

Any prepared rice salad from the delicatessen counter will be suitable for this dish. We chose a nutty, brown-rice variety. Ask your fishmonger to skin and fillet the fish for you.

SERVES 4

two 225 g (8 oz) trout, skinned and filleted
125 g (4 oz) smoked salmon pâté
50 g (2 oz) ready-made rice salad
10 ml (2 tsp) lemon juice
two 25.5 × 51 cm (10 × 20 inch) sheets of filo pastry, thawed if frozen
25 g (1 oz) butter or margarine, melted
sesame seeds
lemon wedges, to garnish

1 Lay the trout fillets flat on a board, skin-side down, and cut each one in half. Divide the smoked salmon pâté between four of the trout pieces and spread evenly to cover them completely.

2 Spoon the rice salad down the centre of the trout pieces on top of the pâté. Sprinkle with lemon juice. Top with the remaining four pieces of trout fillet and press down lightly.

3 Cut each sheet of filo pastry in half and brush with a little butter or margarine. Place a filled trout portion in the centre of one edge of each filo sheet. Fold in the pastry edges and roll up to enclose the trout completely.

4 Place the rolls on a baking sheet, seam-side down, and brush with more melted butter or margarine. Sprinkle generously with sesame seeds and bake in the oven at 200°C (400°F) mark 6 for 20–25 minutes or until golden brown and crisp. Garnish with lemon and serve.

NOT SUITABLE FOR FREEZING

400 Calories per serving

*M*EAT IN MINUTES

*P*EPPERED BEEF SAUTÉ

PREPARATION TIME: 10 minutes
COOKING TIME: 10 minutes

SERVES 2–3

350 g (12 oz) sirloin steaks
15 ml (1 tbsp) olive oil
25 g (1 oz) butter
175 g (6 oz) red onions, skinned and thinly sliced
10 ml (2 level tsp) green peppercorns in brine, drained and finely chopped
90 ml (6 tbsp) single cream
15 ml (1 tsp) lemon juice
salt
lemon slices, to garnish
fine noodles tossed with chives, to serve

1 Cut the steaks into fine, thin strips.
2 Heat the oil and butter together in a medium-sized sauté pan. Add the onion and fry for 3–4 minutes or until just beginning to soften.
3 Stir in the beef and peppercorns, and cook over a high heat for 2–3 minutes or until the meat is tender, stirring frequently.
4 Lower the heat and stir in the cream and lemon juice with salt to taste. Garnish with lemon slices and serve with noodles tossed with chives.

NOT SUITABLE FOR FREEZING

511 Calories per serving

*B*EEF IN REDCURRANT AND WINE SAUCE

PREPARATION TIME: 10 minutes
COOKING TIME: 10 minutes

SERVES 6

550 g (1¼ lb) beef fillet
salt and pepper
30 ml (2 tbsp) oil
3 shallots, skinned and finely chopped
75 g (3 oz) smoked streaky bacon, chopped
20 pink peppercorns in brine, drained and lightly crushed (optional)
175 ml (6 fl oz) red wine
50 ml (2 fl oz) beef stock
15 ml (1 tbsp) lemon juice
a pinch of freshly grated nutmeg
30 ml (2 level tbsp) redcurrant jelly

1 Cut the beef into six even slices. Season.
2 Heat the oil in a large pan and seal the beef slices. Remove and keep warm.
3 Add the shallots and bacon to the pan and sauté for 3–4 minutes. Mix in the peppercorns, if using, wine, stock, lemon juice and nutmeg. Bring to the boil, stir in the redcurrant jelly until dissolved, and season to taste.
4 Replace the meat in the pan, cover and simmer for a further 2–3 minutes.

NOT SUITABLE FOR FREEZING

230 Calories per serving

STEAK AND STILTON PARCELS

PREPARATION TIME: 15 minutes
COOKING TIME: 15–20 minutes

Quick-fry steaks are a real boon for anyone with a hectic schedule. They can quickly be turned into a nutritious and economical meal. If necessary, bat out the steaks with a rolling pin until they are about 0.5 cm (¼ inch) thick.

SERVES 4

2 quick-fry steaks, about 350-450 g (12 oz-1 lb) total weight
oil
75 g (3 oz) blue Stilton cheese
15 ml (1 level tbsp) chopped fresh tarragon or 2.5 ml (½ level tsp) dried
60 ml (4 tbsp) single cream
black pepper
5 large sheets of filo pastry, about 45.5 × 25.5 cm (18 × 10 inches) each, thawed if frozen
50 g (2 oz) butter, melted
lemon juice and mixed-leaf salad, to serve

1 Halve each steak. Heat the oil in a frying pan, add the steaks and cook quickly over a high heat to seal. Remove from the pan and leave to cool.

2 Grate or crumble the cheese, or soften by mashing with a fork. Mix with the tarragon, cream and black pepper (the Stilton should add sufficient salt). Spread the mixture over the cold steaks.

3 Lay one of the filo sheets on a work surface and brush with melted butter. Place a steak on top and wrap the pastry round to enclose it completely, like a parcel. Place on a baking sheet and brush with butter. Repeat with the remaining steaks and three more filo sheets to make four parcels in all.

4 Brush the last sheet of filo with butter and fold it over and over to form a strip about 2.5 cm (1 inch) wide. Cut into diamond shapes and use to decorate the parcels. Brush with melted butter. Chill for about 20 minutes.

5 Bake the parcels in the oven at 220°C (425°F) mark 7 for 15–20 minutes or until well browned. Squeeze lemon juice over the parcels and serve with a mixed-leaf salad.

NOT SUITABLE FOR FREEZING

605 Calories per serving

Steak and Stilton Parcels; Peppered Beef Sauté (page 21)

*O*ATY BEEF BURGERS

PREPARATION TIME: 10 minutes
COOKING TIME: 8 minutes

Oats add valuable fibre to these tasty burgers.

SERVES 4

45 ml (3 level tbsp) tomato chutney
450 g (1 lb) lean minced beef
50 g (2 oz) rolled oats
5 ml (1 level tsp) dried mixed herbs
salt and pepper
1 egg, beaten
oil
warm burger buns, to serve

1 In a medium bowl, mix together the chutney, beef, oats and herbs. Add salt and pepper to taste, and enough beaten egg to bind the mixture.
2 With lightly floured hands, shape the mixture into four or eight flat burgers.
3 Brush each one lightly with oil, and grill for about 4 minutes on each side or until golden and cooked through. The cooking time will depend on the thickness of the burgers.
4 Serve in warm burger buns.

SUITABLE FOR FREEZING

380 Calories per serving

*Q*UICK CHILLI TACOS

PREPARATION TIME: 10 minutes
COOKING TIME: 20–25 minutes

SERVES 4

450 g (1 lb) lean minced beef
125 g (4 oz) onion, skinned and chopped
1 garlic clove, skinned and crushed
1 green pepper, deseeded and chopped
397 g (14 oz) can chopped tomatoes
397 g (14 oz) can red kidney beans, drained and rinsed
15 ml (1 level tbsp) tomato purée
2.5 ml (½ level tsp) chilli powder
15 ml (1 level tbsp) ground cumin
salt and pepper
300 ml (½ pint) water
8 taco shells
125 g (4 oz) Cheddar cheese, grated
60 ml (4 tbsp) soured cream
mixed salad leaves, to serve

1 Place the beef, onion, garlic and green pepper in a large saucepan and heat gently, stirring, until the mince is beginning to brown and the vegetables soften.
2 Add the tomatoes, beans, tomato purée, chilli powder and cumin, and season with salt and pepper. Add the water and stir well. Simmer for 15–20 minutes or until well reduced.
3 Just before serving, heat the taco shells in the oven at 150°C (300°F) mark 2 for 2–3 minutes or until crisp. Spoon a little mince into each taco shell and top with cheese and soured cream. Serve with salad leaves.

SAUCE SUITABLE FOR FREEZING

470 Calories per serving

SPICED COCONUT LAMB

PREPARATION TIME: 5 minutes
COOKING TIME: 25 minutes

SERVES 4

125 g (4 oz) onions, skinned and roughly chopped
1 red chilli, deseeded
30 ml (2 tbsp) oil
2 garlic cloves, skinned
25 g (1 oz) blanched almonds
2.5 ml (½ level tsp) ground turmeric
2.5 ml (½ level tsp) ground ginger
8 lean lamb cutlets, about 450 g (1 lb) total weight
juice of 1 lemon
1 lemon grass stalk
5 ml (1 level tsp) dark muscovado sugar
225 ml (8 fl oz) coconut milk
150 ml (¼ pint) water
salt and pepper
coriander sprigs, to garnish

1 Put the onion and chilli in a food processor or blender with the oil, garlic, nuts and spices, and blend to a paste.

2 Fry the paste in a large frying pan or wok, stirring constantly, for 1–2 minutes. Add the cutlets and cook over a medium heat until well browned on both sides.

3 Add the lemon juice, lemon grass, muscovado sugar, coconut milk and water. Bring to the boil, cover and simmer gently for about 15 minutes or until the cutlets are tender. Uncover and bubble down the juices for 3–4 minutes, to give a coating consistency.

4 Remove the lemon grass and add salt and pepper to taste. Serve garnished with coriander sprigs.

NOT SUITABLE FOR FREEZING

590 Calories per serving

SPICY CINNAMON LAMB

PREPARATION TIME: 10 minutes
COOKING TIME: 20–25 minutes

Serve this oriental-style lamb dish with steamed rice.

SERVES 4

15 ml (1 tbsp) oil
225 g (8 oz) onions, skinned and finely chopped
2 garlic cloves, skinned and crushed
2.5 cm (1 inch) piece of fresh root ginger,
peeled and chopped
700 g (1½ lb) lean fillet or leg of lamb, sliced
into bite-sized pieces
227 g (8 oz) can chopped tomatoes
30 ml (2 tbsp) dark soy sauce
10 ml (2 level tsp) dark muscovado sugar
1.25 ml (¼ level tsp) freshly grated nutmeg
5 ml (1 level tsp) ground cinnamon
pepper
150 ml (¼ pint) water
spring onion shreds, to garnish

1 Heat the oil in a large sauté pan, add the onion, garlic and ginger, and cook for 2–3 minutes or until softened. Add the meat to the pan and cook over a high heat for 4–5 minutes or until the meat is well browned.

2 Stir in the remaining ingredients and bring to the boil. Reduce the heat, cover and simmer gently for about 20 minutes or until the meat is tender. Serve immediately, garnished with spring onion shreds.

NOT SUITABLE FOR FREEZING

510 Calories per serving

*L*AMB FILLET AND PEPPER STIR-FRY

PREPARATION TIME: 10 minutes
COOKING TIME: 12 minutes

The Garlic and Spring Onion Sauce used in this recipe is produced commercially and available bottled from supermarkets.

SERVES 4

30 ml (2 tbsp) oil
450 g (1 lb) lamb fillet, thinly sliced
125 g (4 oz) carrots, peeled and sliced into thin batons
2 celery sticks, trimmed and thinly sliced
1 red pepper, deseeded and sliced
1 yellow pepper, deseeded and sliced
125 g (4 oz) mangetouts
1 large courgette, sliced
45 ml (3 tbsp) Garlic and Spring Onion Sauce
15 ml (1 tbsp) soy sauce
salt and pepper

1 Heat the oil in a large sauté pan or wok and quickly fry the lamb for about 5 minutes or until well cooked through and golden brown. Remove from the pan with a slotted spoon and drain on absorbent kitchen paper.
2 Add the carrots, celery and peppers to the pan and stir-fry for 3–4 minutes. Add all the remaining ingredients together with the lamb. Cook for a further 2–3 minutes or until the vegetables are just tender. Grind black pepper over the dish just before serving.

NOT SUITABLE FOR FREEZING

275 Calories per serving

*L*AMB WITH GARLIC AND COURGETTES

PREPARATION TIME: 10 minutes
COOKING TIME: 20 minutes

SERVES 6

12 large garlic cloves
450 g (1 lb) courgettes, sliced
olive oil
salt and pepper
6 lamb loin chops, about 175 g (6 oz) each, trimmed of fat
6 long sprigs of fresh rosemary

1 Cook the unpeeled garlic cloves in boiling water for 5 minutes, then drain and place in the grill pan with the sliced courgettes. Brush with oil and season.
2 Bend the tail of each chop around the eye of the meat. Using a skewer, make a hole horizontally right through the tail and meat of each chop. Thread a sprig of rosemary through each chop to secure. Brush with oil.
3 Grill the garlic and courgettes for 5 minutes, stirring after 2 minutes. Add the lamb chops and grill for 8 minutes on each side. The garlic skin will blacken but the flesh inside will be soft and smoky.

NOT SUITABLE FOR FREEZING

480 Calories per serving

Lamb with Garlic and Courgettes

STIR-FRIED PORK

PREPARATION TIME: 10 minutes
COOKING TIME: 10 minutes

Stir-fry sauces, such as the chilli and tomato sauce used in this recipe, are now readily available from supermarkets.

SERVES 4

450 g (1 lb) pork fillet (tenderloin)
175 g (6 oz) baby sweetcorn
175 g (6 oz) sugar-snap peas
225 g (8 oz) carrots, peeled and cut into small sticks
salt and pepper
45 ml (3 tbsp) sunflower oil
60 ml (4 tbsp) stir-fry chilli and tomato sauce
5 ml (1 level tsp) caster sugar
30 ml (2 tbsp) wine vinegar
60 ml (4 tbsp) light soy sauce
fresh chives and sprigs of fresh parsley, to garnish

1 Trim the pork and cut across into thin 0.5 cm (¼ inch) slices. Blanch the vegetables in boiling salted water for 2 minutes, then drain and refresh under cold running water.
2 Heat the oil in a wok or large frying pan, preferably non-stick. Add the pork and stir-fry over a high heat for 2–3 minutes or until well browned and almost tender.
3 Add the vegetables and continue stirring over a high heat for 2–3 minutes or until piping hot.
4 Mix in the remaining ingredients and bring to the boil, stirring well. Adjust the seasoning and serve, garnished with chives and sprigs of parsley.

NOT SUITABLE FOR FREEZING

380 Calories per serving

DIJON-GLAZED PORK MEDALLIONS

PREPARATION TIME: 10 minutes
COOKING TIME: 20–25 minutes

Fillet of pork is a lean and tender choice for a special meal. In this dish it is cut into medallions and beaten out to form thin rounds (which cook quickly). Veal escalopes could be used instead of pork, if wished.

SERVES 8

1.4 kg (3 lb) pork fillet (tenderloin)
salt and pepper
15 ml (1 tbsp) vegetable oil
1 onion, skinned and finely chopped
1 garlic clove, skinned and crushed
65 g (2½ oz) butter
45 ml (3 tbsp) Madeira or Marsala
450 ml (¾ pint) chicken stock
15 ml (1 tbsp) Dijon mustard
175 g (6 oz) crème fraîche
25 ml (1½ level tbsp) plain flour
fresh sage leaves, shredded, to garnish

1 Using a sharp knife, slice each pork fillet into 1 cm (½ inch) thick diagonal slices. Put the slices between two sheets of greaseproof paper and, using a meat mallet or rolling pin, pound the slices firmly until they are thin. Sprinkle with salt and pepper.
2 Heat the oil in a large frying pan and gently fry the onion and garlic for about 5 minutes, then remove from the pan. Add 50 g (2 oz) butter to the pan and fry the madallions, a few at a time, for 2–3 minutes or until the pork is just cooked on each side. Remove from the pan and keep warm while cooking the remainder in the same way. Remove from the pan and keep warm.
3 Add the Madeira to the pan and stir in the onion mixture, stock, mustard and crème fraîche. Bring to the boil and boil rapidly for

about 4 minutes or until partially reduced. Meanwhile, mix together the remaining butter and the flour to form a paste. Gradually add to the sauce, stirring all the time. Boil for 2 minutes, stirring until the sauce has thickened.

4 Return the pork to the pan and heat through for 2 minutes, spooning the sauce over during heating. Serve garnished with sage.

NOT SUITABLE FOR FREEZING

445 Calories per serving

Pork and Coriander Stir-Fry

PREPARATION TIME: 5 minutes
COOKING TIME: 15 minutes

This quick and easy stir-fry meal combines tender, succulent pieces of lean pork fillet with fresh, crunchy vegetables. Serve with a simple accompaniment, such as plain steamed rice.

SERVES 4

350 g (12 oz) pork fillet (tenderloin)
30 ml (2 tbsp) oil
6 celery sticks, trimmed and cut into thin sticks
175 g (6 oz) onions, skinned and finely diced
10 ml (2 level tsp) ground coriander
90 ml (6 tbsp) apple juice
salt and pepper
125 g (4 oz) beansprouts
45 ml (3 level tbsp) chopped fresh coriander

1 Thinly slice the pork fillet, discarding any fat or sinew.

2 Heat 15 ml (1 tbsp) oil in a large non-stick frying or sauté pan, add the pork and brown lightly. Drain on absorbent kitchen paper.

3 Heat the remaining oil in the pan and add the celery, onion and ground coriander. Stir-fry for 1–2 minutes.

4 Pour in the apple juice with 45 ml (3 tbsp) water. Replace the pork, add salt and pepper to taste, cover and simmer for 5 minutes.

5 Uncover, stir in the beansprouts and fresh coriander and cook over a high heat for 2–3 minutes, stirring every now and then. The ingredients should be just tender and the pan juices well reduced. Adjust the seasoning and serve.

NOT SUITABLE FOR FREEZING

230 Calories per serving

VARIATION

Use chopped fresh parsley instead of coriander.

Pork in Mustard

PREPARATION TIME: 10 minutes
COOKING TIME: 15 minutes

Mushrooms and mustard together are delicious combined with pork and pasta. If you prefer to use whole-wheat pasta, remember that it will take longer to cook. Follow the packet instructions and use plenty of boiling, salted water in a large saucepan. Add 2.5 ml (½ tsp) olive oil to stop the pasta sticking while cooking, if wished.

SERVES 4

175 g (6 oz) dried pasta shapes, e.g. cappelletti
salt and pepper
450 g (1 lb) pork fillet (tenderloin)
olive oil
2 garlic cloves, skinned and crushed
50 g (2 oz) butter
225 g (8 oz) button mushrooms, wiped and sliced
30 ml (2 level tbsp) wholegrain mustard
60 ml (4 level tbsp) chopped fresh chives

1 Cook the pasta in boiling, salted water according to packet instructions or until just tender.

2 Meanwhile, trim the pork fillet, discarding any fat, and cut into very thin (0.5 cm/¼ inch) slices.

3 Heat 45 ml (3 tbsp) oil with the garlic in a large sauté pan, preferably non-stick. Add the pork, a little at a time, and brown well over a high heat for 2–3 minutes. Remove with a slotted spoon. Continue until all the meat is browned.

4 Add the butter, mushrooms and mustard to the pan, and sauté, stirring, for about 2 minutes. Drain the pasta well and toss in a little olive oil.

5 Add the pork and the pasta to the sauté pan. Continue to stir together over a high heat until the mixture is piping hot.

6 Adjust the seasoning and serve immediately, garnished with chopped fresh chives.

NOT SUITABLE FOR FREEZING

550 Calories per serving

VARIATION

For a richer flavour, try adding dried mushrooms. You'll find dried *porcini* mushrooms in most large supermarkets and good delicatessens. Soak according to the packet instructions, then drain and stir into the pasta at step 4.

Pork in Mustard

PORK FILLET WITH APPLE

PREPARATION TIME: 15 minutes
COOKING TIME: 15 minutes

*Apples always combine well with pork as their fruiti-
ness offsets the rich meat. Use firm, crisp apples, such
as Granny Smiths, or they may break up when cooking.*

SERVES 4

30 ml (2 tbsp) oil
550 g (1¼ lb) pork fillet (tenderloin), thinly sliced
10 ml (2 level tsp) ground coriander
300 ml (½ pint) cider
150 ml (¼ pint) stock
75 g (3 oz) frozen baby onions
2 apples, peeled, cored and sliced
45 ml (3 level tbsp) chopped fresh parsley
150 ml (5 fl oz) single cream
salt and pepper

1 Heat the oil in a large shallow sauté pan and
brown the pork in two batches, adding a little
more oil if necessary.
2 Return all the meat to the pan and add the
coriander, cider, stock, frozen onions and
apple slices. Bring to the boil and simmer for
about 5 minutes or until the pork and onions
are tender.
3 Stir in the chopped parsley and cream. Simmer gently for a further 1–2 minutes to heat
through. Add salt and pepper to taste, and
serve.

NOT SUITABLE FOR FREEZING

380 Calories per serving

FRENCH-STYLE SAUSAGES WITH LENTILS

PREPARATION TIME: 5 minutes
COOKING TIME: 25 minutes

SERVES 4

30 ml (2 tbsp) oil
450 g (1 lb) good-quality chunky sausages,
skinned and sliced
6 large garlic cloves, skinned
350 g (12 oz) small brown or green lentils
225 g (8 oz) parsnips
about 900 ml (1½ pints) chicken or vegetable
stock
salt and pepper
finely chopped spring onions, to garnish

1 Heat the oil in a medium saucepan, preferably non-stick, and fry the sausage and garlic
for 3–4 minutes or until golden.
2 Meanwhile, rinse and drain the lentils. Peel
the parsnips and cut into large chunks.
3 Add the lentils and parsnips to the saucepan
with the stock. Add salt and pepper to taste,
and bring to the boil. Reduce the heat, cover
and simmer for about 20 minutes or until the
lentils are tender and much of the liquid has
been absorbed, adding a little more stock if
necessary.
4 Adjust the seasoning and serve garnished
with spring onions.

NOT SUITABLE FOR FREEZING

770 Calories per serving

Herb SAUSAGES WITH CARAMELISED ONIONS

PREPARATION TIME: 5–10 minutes

COOKING TIME: 25 minutes

SERVES 4

25 g (1 oz) butter
30 ml (2 tbsp) olive oil
350 g (12 oz) button onions, skinned, or
4 onions, skinned and roughly chopped
30 ml (2 level tbsp) caster sugar
450 g (1 lb) good-quality pork sausagemeat
15–30 ml (1–2 level tbsp) chopped fresh herbs,
e.g. marjoram, thyme, oregano, etc.
15 ml (1 level tbsp) Dijon mustard
salt and pepper

1 Heat the butter and olive oil in a frying pan. Add the onions and sugar and stir well, then reduce the heat slightly. Cover and cook for about 15 minutes or until the onions are just tender. Do not lift the lid too often or the onions will stick.

2 Meanwhile, use a fork to mix together the sausagemeat, herbs, mustard and salt and pepper to taste. Shape into 12 sausages or small, flat rounds. Grill for about 10 minutes or until cooked through, turning as necessary.

3 Serve the sausages with the caramelised onions.

NOT SUITABLE FOR FREEZING

570 Calories per serving

Perfect PILAFF

PREPARATION TIME: 5 minutes

COOKING TIME: 20 minutes

SERVES 4

350 g (12 oz) lamb's liver
30 ml (2 tbsp) oil
175 g (6 oz) onion, skinned and thinly sliced
1 green pepper, deseeded and thinly sliced
30 ml (2 level tbsp) sunflower seeds
225 g (8 oz) long-grain white rice
about 450 ml (¾ pint) light stock
30 ml (2 tbsp) lemon juice
1 garlic clove, skinned and crushed
salt and pepper
chopped fresh parsley

1 Trim the liver and slice into fine strips. Heat the oil in a large flameproof casserole or heavy-based sauté pan, add the liver and brown quickly. Lift out of the pan using a slotted spoon, and drain on absorbent kitchen paper.

2 Add the onion and pepper to the pan together with the sunflower seeds, and stir-fry for 1–2 minutes.

3 Mix in the rice followed by the stock, lemon juice, garlic and salt and pepper to taste. Bring to the boil, cover tightly and simmer for 10 minutes.

4 Stir in the liver, re-cover and simmer for about 5 minutes longer, or until the rice is tender and most of the liquid has been absorbed. Adjust the seasoning, stirring in plenty of chopped parsley.

NOT SUITABLE FOR FREEZING

480 Calories per serving

PEPPERONI PAN PIZZA

PREPARATION TIME: 10 minutes

COOKING TIME: 15 minutes

This recipe uses scone mixture for a faster pizza base. Try adding some chopped fresh herbs to the dough too.

SERVES 4

125 g (4 oz) self-raising wholemeal flour
125 g (4 oz) self-raising white flour
salt and pepper
5 ml (1 level tsp) baking powder
5 ml (1 level tsp) mustard powder
40 g (1½ oz) butter or margarine
about 150 ml (¼ pint) milk
olive oil
30 ml (2 level tbsp) tomato purée
400 g (14 oz) can chopped tomatoes
50 g (2 oz) mushrooms, wiped and sliced
3 thin salami snack sticks (pepperoni), about 75 g (3 oz) total weight, sliced
6 pitted black olives, halved
15 ml (1 level tbsp) chopped fresh thyme or 5 ml (1 level tsp) dried
225 g (8 oz) Cheddar cheese, grated

1 Put the flours, a pinch of salt, the baking powder and mustard in a bowl, and mix well. Rub in the butter or margarine, then add enough milk to make a soft dough. Knead lightly on a floured surface, then roll out into a round to fit a large oiled frying pan, about 21.5 cm (8½ inches).

2 Cook the dough gently in the pan for 3–5 minutes or until the base is golden. Turn out on to a baking sheet, then slide back into the pan, uncooked-side down.

3 Spread tomato purée over the dough and arrange the tomatoes, mushrooms, pepperoni, olives and thyme over the top. Season well with salt and pepper, and drizzle with oil.

4 Continue to cook until the underside is golden, then transfer the pan to the grill and cook the pizza for a further 5 minutes. Serve immediately.

NOT SUITABLE FOR FREEZING

600 Calories per serving

SPICED LIVER SAUTÉ

PREPARATION TIME: 10 minutes

COOKING TIME: 15 minutes

If fresh fine green beans are not available, use frozen.

SERVES 4

450 g (1 lb) lamb's liver
oil
125 g (4 oz) onion, skinned and sliced
125 g (4 oz) button mushrooms, wiped and sliced if necessary
125 g (4 oz) fine green beans
15 ml (1 level tbsp) plain flour
5–10 ml (1–2 level tsp) paprika
150 ml (¼ pint) light stock
Tabasco sauce
salt and pepper
150 ml (5 fl oz) single cream

1 Wash and trim the liver and cut into strips. Heat 30 ml (2 tbsp) oil in a large sauté pan, add the liver and fry until browned. Lift out with a draining spoon and set aside, keeping it warm.

2 Add the onion, mushrooms and beans to the pan, with a little more oil if necessary, and cook, stirring, until beginning to soften. Mix in the flour and paprika and cook for a further 1 minute.

3 Add the stock and liver to the pan with Tabasco and salt and pepper to taste. Simmer, covered, for 5–10 minutes or until the liver is cooked and the vegetables are just tender.

4 Stir in the cream, adjust the seasoning and bubble up quickly before serving.

NOT SUITABLE FOR FREEZING

350 Calories per serving

Sautéed Liver with Sage and Apple

PREPARATION TIME: 5 minutes
COOKING TIME: 10 minutes

SERVES 4

450 g (1 lb) calves' liver, trimmed and thinly sliced
25 g (1 oz) plain flour
45 ml (3 tbsp) oil
125 g (4 oz) leeks, trimmed and sliced
5 ml (1 level tsp) dried rubbed sage or dried mixed herbs
15 ml (1 level tbsp) mustard, preferably wholegrain
150 ml (5 fl oz) single cream

300 ml (½ pint) apple juice
salt and pepper

1 Cut the liver into small pieces. Sprinkle the flour on to a flat plate and coat the liver pieces well on all sides.
2 Heat 30 ml (2 tbsp) oil in a large sauté pan (preferably non-stick) and brown the liver well for about 30 seconds on each side. Remove with a slotted spoon.
3 Add the remaining oil, leeks and herbs to the pan. Sauté, stirring well, for 2–3 minutes. Mix in the mustard, cream and apple juice, then bring to the boil and bubble for about 5 minutes or until the sauce is reduced by about half.
4 Return the liver to the pan with salt and pepper to taste, and simmer for 1–2 minutes or until heated through. Serve immediately.

NOT SUITABLE FOR FREEZING

410 Calories per serving

VARIATION

Sauté a little thinly sliced eating apple with the leeks for added texture and colour.

QUICK CHICKEN AND DUCK

CHICKEN WITH OYSTER SAUCE

PREPARATION TIME: 10 minutes
COOKING TIME: 15 minutes

SERVES 4

450 g (1 lb) skinless chicken breast fillets
90 ml (6 tbsp) oil
45 ml (3 tbsp) oyster sauce
15 ml (1 tbsp) dark soy sauce
100 ml (4 fl oz) chicken stock
10 ml (2 tsp) lemon juice
1 garlic clove, skinned and finely sliced
6–8 large flat mushrooms, about 250 g (9 oz)
total weight, wiped and sliced
125 g (4 oz) mangetouts
5 ml (1 level tsp) cornflour
15 ml (1 tbsp) sesame oil
salt and pepper

1 Slice the chicken into bite-sized pieces. Heat 45 ml (3 tbsp) oil in a wok or large frying pan, add the chicken and cook over a high heat, stirring continuously for 2–3 minutes or until lightly browned. Remove with a slotted spoon and drain on absorbent kitchen paper.
2 Mix the oyster sauce, soy sauce, chicken stock and lemon juice together in a bowl. Add the chicken and stir until thoroughly combined.
3 Heat the remaining oil over a high heat, add the garlic and stir-fry for about 30 seconds. Add the mushrooms and cook for 1 minute. Add the chicken mixture, cover and simmer for 8 minutes.
4 Stir in the mangetouts and cook for a further 2–3 minutes. Mix the cornflour with 15 ml (1 tbsp) water. Remove the wok or frying pan from the heat and stir in the cornflour mixture. Return to the heat, add the sesame oil and stir until the sauce has thickened. Adjust the seasoning and serve.

NOT SUITABLE FOR FREEZING

410 Calories per serving

Chicken with Oyster Sauce

BAKED CHICKEN FILLETS WITH PESTO

PREPARATION TIME: 5 minutes
COOKING TIME: 25 minutes

SERVES 4

4 skinless chicken breast fillets, about 450 g
(1 lb) total weight
125 g (4 oz) low-fat soft cheese
30 ml (2 level tbsp) pesto sauce
salt and pepper
4 thin slices of ham
shredded basil, to garnish

1 Make a deep cut horizontally in each chicken fillet to form a pocket.
2 Mix together the cheese and pesto, and add salt and pepper to taste. Spoon most of the mixture into the 'pockets'. Wrap a slice of ham around each fillet.
3 Place the chicken fillets on individual pieces of foil and spoon over the remaining cheese mixture. Wrap the foil around the chicken and seal to make parcels.
4 Place on a baking sheet and cook in the oven at 200°C (400°F) mark 6 for 25 minutes or until the chicken is tender.
5 Serve the chicken and juices garnished with shredded basil.

NOT SUITABLE FOR FREEZING

255 Calories per serving

SPICED CHICKEN WITH GRAPES

PREPARATION TIME: 5 minutes
COOKING TIME: 25 minutes

SERVES 4

30 ml (2 tbsp) oil
8 chicken thighs with bone, about 800 g (1¾ lb)
total weight, skinned
175 g (6 oz) onion, skinned and sliced
1 garlic clove, skinned and crushed
5 ml (1 level tsp) ground coriander
5 ml (1 level tsp) ground cumin
a pinch of ground turmeric
150 ml (¼ pint) chicken stock
salt and pepper
125 g (4 oz) seedless green grapes
150 g (5 oz) natural yogurt

1 Heat the oil in a large sauté pan and brown the chicken on both sides. Drain on absorbent kitchen paper.
2 Reduce the heat and cook the onion and garlic with the spices for 2–3 minutes, stirring often.
3 Return the chicken to the pan with the stock and salt and pepper to taste. Bring to the boil, then reduce the heat, cover and simmer gently for about 20 minutes.
4 Meanwhile, halve the grapes if large. Stir the grapes into the chicken juices with the yogurt. Heat through gently and adjust the seasoning.

SUITABLE FOR FREEZING AT THE END OF STEP 3

360 Calories per serving

Lemon Chicken Kebabs

PREPARATION TIME: 10–15 minutes

COOKING TIME: 20 minutes

SERVES 4

juice of 1 lemon
15 ml (1 tbsp) olive oil
1 garlic clove, skinned and crushed
salt and pepper
8 boned and skinned chicken thighs, about
350 g (12 oz) total weight
1 small red pepper, deseeded and cut into
bite-sized pieces
225 g (8 oz) small courgettes, thickly sliced
1 green eating apple, cored and thickly sliced
450 g (1 lb) leeks, trimmed and shredded
25 g (1 oz) butter or margarine

1 Mix together the lemon juice, oil, garlic and seasoning. Cut each chicken thigh in half and place in the lemon mixture. Stir and leave to marinate for about 15 minutes.

2 Thread the chicken, pepper, courgettes and apple on to skewers and brush with the lemon marinade. Grill for 15–20 minutes, turning and basting with the marinade.

3 Meanwhile, put the leeks in a saucepan with the butter or margarine and 30 ml (2 tbsp) water. Cover and simmer for about 15 minutes or until tender. Season with plenty of black pepper.

4 Serve the kebabs on a bed of leeks.

NOT SUITABLE FOR FREEZING

280 Calories per serving

Brandied Chicken

PREPARATION TIME: 10–15 minutes

COOKING TIME: 20 minutes

This is surprisingly low in calories for such a deliciously creamy dish.

SERVES 4

25 g (1 oz) butter
4 skinless chicken breast fillets, about 125 g
(4 oz) each
75 g (3 oz) shallots or onion, skinned and
finely chopped
200 ml (7 fl oz) lager
25 ml (1 fl oz) brandy
175 g (6 oz) button mushrooms, wiped
50 ml (2 fl oz) double cream
salt and pepper
flat-leafed parsley, to garnish

1 Melt the butter in a flameproof casserole. Add the chicken breasts, two at a time, and fry until browned. Remove with a slotted spoon.

2 Stir the shallots or onion into the fat remaining in the pan, and sauté for 1–2 minutes. Return all the chicken to the pan with the lager, brandy and mushrooms. Bring to the boil, cover and simmer for about 20 minutes or until the chicken is very tender.

3 Remove the chicken to a warmed serving dish and cover with foil. Boil the cooking liquor until reduced by half. Stir in the cream, season with salt and pepper, and pour over the chicken to cover completely. Garnish with parsley and serve.

NOT SUITABLE FOR FREEZING

285 Calories per serving

SPICY CHICKEN WITH CASHEWS

PREPARATION TIME: 5–10 minutes
COOKING TIME: 25 minutes

Serve this flavoursome chicken dish with plain green vegetables and steamed or boiled rice. Try serving a mixture of rice for a change. Packets of easy-cook mixed rice are available from supermarkets.

SERVES 4

25 g (1 oz) piece of fresh root ginger, peeled and sliced

4 garlic cloves, skinned, or 10 ml (2 level tsp) garlic purée

50 g (2 oz) unsalted cashew nuts

150 g (5 oz) natural yogurt

oil

700 g (1½ lb) chicken thighs with bone, skinned

125 g (4 oz) onion, skinned and chopped

2 bay leaves

10 ml (2 level tsp) ground cumin

small pinch of cayenne pepper

200 ml (7 fl oz) stock

salt and pepper

30 ml (2 level tbsp) chopped fresh coriander or parsley

coriander or parsley sprigs, to garnish

1 Put the ginger, garlic, nuts, and 30 ml (2 level tbsp) yogurt in a blender or food processor and purée to a rough paste.

2 Heat a little oil in a large, shallow, flame-proof casserole and brown the chicken. Remove from the pan. Stir the onion into the oil remaining in the pan and add the nut paste, bay leaves and spices. Cook, stirring, for 1–2 minutes. Add the remaining yogurt, the stock and salt and pepper to taste. Bring to the boil.

3 Return the chicken to the pan, cover and simmer for 25 minutes or until the chicken is quite tender, stirring occasionally.

4 Mix in the chopped coriander or parsley and season to taste before serving. Garnish with sprigs of coriander or parsley.

NOT SUITABLE FOR FREEZING

360 Calories per serving

POACHED CHICKEN IN WATERCRESS SAUCE

PREPARATION TIME: 5 minutes
COOKING TIME: 15 minutes

Serve this unusual chicken dish with lightly sautéed chanterelle mushrooms.

SERVES 4

4 skinless chicken breast fillets, each weighing about 125 g (4 oz)

4 thin slices of Parma ham

90 ml (6 tbsp) dry white wine

50 ml (2 fl oz) chicken stock

60 ml (4 tbsp) single cream

90 ml (6 level tbsp) chopped watercress

black pepper

flat-leaf parsley, to garnish

1 Wrap each chicken breast in a slice of ham. Place in a saucepan just large enough to take the chicken in one layer.

2 Pour the wine and stock over the chicken and bring to the boil. Reduce the heat, cover and simmer gently for 10–12 minutes or until the chicken is tender. Remove the chicken to a serving dish and keep warm.

3 Bring the pan juices to the boil and bubble to reduce to about 75 ml (5 tbsp). Add the cream and return to the boil. Take off the heat and mix in the watercress. Season well with

pepper and pour over the chicken. Garnish with parsley and serve.

NOT SUITABLE FOR FREEZING

215 Calories per serving

Poached Chicken in Watercress Sauce

VARIATION

To serve cold, complete to the end of step 2, then cool the chicken and slice thickly. Fold the watercress into 60 ml (4 level tbsp) mayonnaise and serve with the chicken.

CHICKEN WITH BASIL SAUCE

PREPARATION TIME: 10 minutes
COOKING TIME: 16 minutes

SERVES 4

a bunch of fresh basil, about 50 g (2 oz)
4 chicken breasts with skin, about 175 g
(6 oz) each
6 anchovy fillets
60 ml (4 tbsp) red wine vinegar
20 ml (4 level tsp) Dijon mustard
175 ml (6 fl oz) olive oil
pasta, to serve

1 Carefully push 2–3 basil leaves under the skin of each chicken breast.
2 Place the remaining basil leaves, anchovy fillets, red wine vinegar and Dijon mustard in a food processor and blend until the mixture becomes quite smooth. With the motor still running, slowly pour in the olive oil. Transfer the mixture to a small bowl.
3 Cook the chicken breasts under a moderate grill for 6–8 minutes on each side, or until they are cooked through. Serve with a few spoonfuls of the basil sauce, and accompanied by pasta.

NOT SUITABLE FOR FREEZING

*400 Calories per serving of chicken;
95 Calories per 15 ml (1 tbsp) sauce*

VARIATION

If you are unable to obtain fresh basil, use 25 g (1 oz) fresh parsley and about 15 ml (1 level tbsp) bought pesto sauce.

CHINESE RICE POT

PREPARATION TIME: 10 minutes
COOKING TIME: 20 minutes

SERVES 4

225 g (8 oz) mixed long-grain and wild rice
450 g (1 lb) skinless chicken breast fillets
350 g (12 oz) broccoli
225 g (8 oz) fresh asparagus or young leeks
45 ml (3 tbsp) olive oil
1 cm (½ inch) piece of fresh root ginger, peeled
and finely chopped
2 garlic cloves, skinned and finely chopped
salt and pepper
chicken or vegetable stock
10 ml (2 tsp) sesame oil
fresh herb sprigs, to garnish

1 Place the rice in a sieve and wash in cold water until the water runs clear. Set aside. Dice the chicken. Cut the broccoli into small florets and the asparagus or leeks into 2.5 cm (1 inch) lengths, discarding any coarse stalks.
2 Heat the olive oil in a large heavy, preferably non-stick, saucepan. Add the ginger, garlic and chicken and stir-fry for 2–3 minutes or until beginning to brown. Add the rice with salt and pepper to taste, and stir well. Pour in enough stock to cover completely – about 600 ml (1 pint) – and bring quickly to the boil.
3 Place the broccoli and asparagus on top of the rice. Cover and simmer for 10 minutes.
4 Stir quickly to mix the vegetables through the rice. Cover and cook for 10 minutes.
5 Fluff up the rice with a fork, sprinkle with sesame oil and garnish wtih fresh herb sprigs.

NOT SUITABLE FOR FREEZING

500 Calories per serving

CHICKEN AND COURGETTE PITTA POCKETS

PREPARATION TIME: 12 minutes
COOKING TIME: 12 minutes

If possible, warm the pittas by placing them under the grill or in the oven.

SERVES 4

90 ml (6 level tbsp) natural yogurt
30 ml (2 level tbsp) wholegrain mustard
juice of 1 large lime
salt and pepper
450 g (1 lb) skinless chicken breast fillets, diced
225 g (8 oz) small courgettes, sliced
2 eating apples
4 small pitta breads
salad leaves, to serve

1 Mix together the yogurt, mustard, lime juice and seasoning. Stir the chicken into the marinade, cover and leave to stand for about 10 minutes, longer if possible.
2 Place the chicken and the marinade in a foil-lined grill pan and grill for about 12 minutes or until cooked through, turning occasionally.
3 Meanwhile, blanch the courgettes in boiling salted water for 1 minute, then drain. Core and slice the apples.
4 Halve each pitta bread and open out to form a pocket. Fill each one with a mixture of chicken, courgettes and apple, and serve with salad leaves.

NOT SUITABLE FOR FREEZING

380 Calories per serving

SPICED CHICKEN AND CHICK PEA POT

PREPARATION TIME: 5–10 minutes
COOKING TIME: 25 minutes

SERVES 4

450 g (1 lb) boneless cooked chicken tikka pieces
425 g (15 oz) can chick pea dhal
50 g (2 oz) creamed coconut, broken up
150 ml (¼ pint) milk
30 ml (2 level tbsp) chopped fresh coriander
two 25.5 × 51 cm (10 × 20 inch) sheets of filo pastry
50 g (2 oz) butter or margarine, melted
5 ml (1 level tsp) cumin seeds

1 Cut the chicken into bite-sized pieces.
2 Heat together the chick pea dhal, creamed coconut and milk until well blended and smooth. Stir in the chicken pieces and coriander, and spoon into a 1.3 litre (2¼ pint) pie dish.
3 Brush the filo pastry sheets with the melted butter and cut into small triangles. Lightly scrunch up the filo pastry pieces and dot over the chicken mixture to cover the surface completely. Sprinkle over the cumin seeds.
4 Bake in the oven at 200°C (400°F) mark 6 for 25–30 minutes or until golden brown and crisp.

NOT SUITABLE FOR FREEZING

665 Calories per serving

VARIATION

Use thinly rolled out shortcrust or puff pastry as an alternative topping.

Spicy Chicken

PREPARATION TIME: 10 minutes
COOKING TIME: 20 minutes

SERVES 4

1 small green chilli, deseeded and finely chopped
about 60 ml (4 level tbsp) chopped fresh
coriander or parsley
75 g (3 oz) butter, softened
salt and pepper
4 chicken breast fillets with skin, about 150 g
(5 oz) each
30 ml (2 tbsp) lemon juice
700 g (1½ lb) pumpkin or squash
225 g (8 oz) French beans
coriander sprigs, to garnish

1 Beat the chilli and coriander or parsley into the butter. Add salt and pepper to taste.
2 Slash each side of the chicken three or four times to a depth of about 0.5 cm (¼ inch) and place, skin-side down, on a grill pan. Spread with half the butter and sprinkle with lemon juice.
3 Grill under a moderate heat for 7 minutes, turn and spread with the remaining butter. Grill for a further 7 minutes. Reserve any melted butter.
4 Meanwhile, peel and cut the pumpkin into bite-sized pieces, discarding the seeds. Cook the pumpkin and the beans together in boiling salted water for 5–10 minutes. Drain well.
5 Serve the chicken with the vegetables, spooning over any reserved butter. Garnish with coriander.

NOT SUITABLE FOR FREEZING

360 Calories per serving

Speedy Risotto

PREPARATION TIME: 5–10 minutes
COOKING TIME: 25 minutes

Cooking the rice with all the other ingredients gives this risotto a rich, full flavour.

SERVES 4

350 g (12 oz) boneless chicken thighs,
skinned and sliced into strips
175 g (6 oz) onion, skinned and chopped
3 tomatoes, chopped
175 g (6 oz) button mushrooms, wiped and
quartered or halved if necessary
1 garlic clove, skinned and crushed
750 ml (1¼ pints) chicken stock
350 g (12 oz) long-grain white rice
1.25 ml (¼ level tsp) ground turmeric
5 ml (1 level tsp) paprika
salt and pepper
175 g (6 oz) cooked peeled prawns
75 g (3 oz) frozen peas
45 ml (3 level tbsp) chopped fresh parsley
lemon slices and whole prawns, to garnish

1 Put the chicken, onion, tomatoes, mushrooms, garlic, stock, rice and spices in a large saucepan. Add salt and pepper to taste and bring to the boil, then reduce the heat, cover and simmer gently for 15–20 minutes or until the chicken is tender, stirring occasionally.
2 Add the prawns and peas and continue to cook, stirring occasionally, for about 5 minutes or until the prawns and peas are heated through. Stir in the parsley and adjust the seasoning. Garnish with lemon slices and prawns.

NOT SUITABLE FOR FREEZING

490 Calories per serving

Spicy Chicken

GLAZED CHICKEN RISOTTO

PREPARATION TIME: 10 minutes
COOKING TIME: 20 minutes

SERVES 4

finely grated rind and juice of 1 orange
finely grated rind and juice of 1 lemon
30 ml (2 tbsp) runny honey
1.25 ml (¼ level tsp) ground turmeric (optional)
12 boned and skinned chicken thighs, about
450 g (1 lb) total weight
50 g (2 oz) spring onions
30 ml (2 tbsp) oil
125 g (4 oz) long-grain white rice
300 ml (½ pint) chicken stock
salt and pepper

1 Mix together the orange and lemon rind, 30 ml (2 tbsp) orange juice, 15 ml (1 tbsp) lemon juice, the honey and turmeric, if using. Add the chicken and stir to coat completely. Thinly slice the spring onions, reserving some of their green tops for garnish.

2 Heat the oil in a frying pan and add the chicken pieces, a few at a time, reserving any leftover honey mixture (watch out as the chicken splutters). Cook each batch until brown.

3 Return all the chicken to the pan and add the remaining ingredients and any excess glaze. Bring to the boil, then reduce the heat, cover and simmer for about 15 minutes or until the rice and chicken are tender and most of the excess liquid has been absorbed.

4 Adjust the seasoning and serve immediately, garnished with spring onion tops.

NOT SUITABLE FOR FREEZING

390 Calories per serving

SESAME STIR-FRY

PREPARATION TIME: 5 minutes
COOKING TIME: 15 minutes

SERVES 4

4 skinless chicken breast fillets, about 450 g
(1 lb) total weight
225 g (8 oz) broccoli
225 g (8 oz) baby sweetcorn
60 ml (4 tbsp) sesame oil
30 ml (2 tbsp) soy sauce
200 ml (7 fl oz) orange juice
salt and pepper
30 ml (2 level tbsp) toasted sesame seeds
50 g (2 oz) unsalted peanuts in skins

1 Cut the chicken into thin strips, the broccoli into small florets and the baby sweetcorn cobs into two or three pieces.

2 Heat the sesame oil in a large frying pan or wok, add the chicken and stir-fry over a high heat for 5–6 minutes or until browned.

3 Stir in the broccoli and sweetcorn, and cook, stirring, for a further 1–2 minutes.

4 Pour over the soy sauce and orange juice and allow the juices to bubble for 3–4 minutes. Adjust the seasoning. Stir in the toasted sesame seeds and unsalted peanuts just before serving.

NOT SUITABLE FOR FREEZING

540 Calories per serving

Duckling and Bacon with Cranberry

PREPARATION TIME: 5–10 minutes

COOKING TIME: 25 minutes

It's quicker to slice the duckling fillets into chunky finger lengths before browning.

SERVES 8

125 g (4 oz) streaky bacon, derinded and roughly chopped
8 duckling breast fillets, skinned
oil
125 g (4 oz) small button mushrooms, wiped and halved if large
450 ml (¾ pint) chicken stock
45 ml (3 level tbsp) cranberry sauce
2.5 ml (½ level tsp) tomato purée
salt and pepper
10 ml (2 level tsp) cornflour

1 Cook the bacon in a shallow flameproof casserole until the fat begins to run. Quickly brown the duckling breasts on both sides, adding a little more oil to the pan if you find it necessary.

2 Stir in the mushrooms, stock, cranberry sauce, tomato purée and salt and pepper to taste. Bring to the boil, cover and cook in the oven at 180°C (350°F) mark 4 for about 25 minutes or until the duckling is tender.

3 Blend the cornflour to a smooth paste with a little cold water and stir it into the casserole. Bring to the boil, adjust the seasoning and serve.

NOT SUITABLE FOR FREEZING

215 Calories per serving

Pan-fried Duck with Spring Greens and Ginger

PREPARATION TIME: 10 minutes

COOKING TIME: 18–20 minutes

SERVES 4

4 small duck breasts, about 175 g (6 oz) each
salt and pepper
2.5 ml (½ level tsp) Chinese five-spice powder
30 ml (2 tbsp) vegetable oil
350 g (12 oz) spring greens, finely shredded
1 bunch of spring onions, trimmed and sliced
2 garlic cloves, skinned and crushed
1 yellow or orange pepper, deseeded and sliced
2 pieces of bottled stem ginger, thinly sliced
15 ml (1 tbsp) syrup from the stem ginger bottle
60 ml (4 tbsp) fresh orange juice
10 ml (2 tsp) white wine vinegar

1 Score the skin of the duck breasts and rub with salt and the five-spice powder.

2 Heat the oil in a frying pan, add the duck and fry quickly on all sides for 4 minutes. Remove from the pan and drain.

3 Add the spring greens, spring onions, garlic and sliced pepper to the pan, and fry quickly, stirring, for 2 minutes or until the greens wilt. Remove from the pan and keep warm.

4 Return the duck to the pan with the ginger, syrup, orange juice and wine vinegar. Cover and cook for 10–12 minutes or until the duck is cooked but still slightly pink in the centre. Season lightly.

5 Transfer the vegetables to warmed serving plates and spoon over the duck and juices.

NOT SUITABLE FOR FREEZING

459 Calories per serving

FISH IN A FLASH

ROLLED PLAICE WITH APPLE

PREPARATION TIME: 15 minutes
COOKING TIME: 10 minutes

SERVES 4

25 g (1 oz) butter or margarine
225 g (8 oz) button mushrooms, wiped
and chopped
125 g (4 oz) eating apple, peeled, cored and
chopped
25 g (1 oz) fresh brown breadcrumbs
5 ml (1 level tsp) wholegrain mustard
30 ml (2 level tbsp) chopped fresh parsley
salt and pepper
4 plaice fillets, about 125 g (4 oz) each, skinned
60 ml (4 tbsp) dry cider
apple slices, to garnish

1 Melt the butter or margarine in a saucepan and sauté the mushrooms and apple for 2–3 minutes. Increase the heat and cook, stirring, for 1–2 minutes or until most of the excess liquid has evaporated. Off the heat, stir in the breadcrumbs, half the mustard and the chopped parsley. Season with salt and pepper.

2 Divide the mixture between the plaice fillets, roll up and secure with wooden cocktail sticks. Place the fish rolls, seam-side down, in a small, shallow flameproof dish.

3 Whisk together the remaining mustard and the cider, and spoon over the fish. Cook under a preheated hot grill for about 10 minutes, turning occasionally and brushing with the mustard mixture. Serve immediately, garnished with apple slices.

NOT SUITABLE FOR FREEZING

210 Calories per serving

Clockwise from top: Rolled Plaice with Apple; Haddock and Soured Cream Gratin (page 50); Seafood Kebabs (page 50)

Seafood Kebabs

PREPARATION TIME: 15 minutes
COOKING TIME: 10 minutes

Serves 4

450 g (1 lb) monkfish or cod fillet
125 g (4 oz) cucumber
1 lemon or lime
50 g (2 oz) large, cooked peeled prawns
75 ml (3 fl oz) vinaigrette with garlic
15 ml (1 level tbsp) chopped fresh dill or 2.5 ml
(½ level tsp) dried
salt and pepper
dill sprigs, to garnish
green salad and crusty bread, to serve

1 Skin the fish if necessary and cut into 2.5 cm (1 inch) cubes. Halve the cucumber lengthways and slice thickly. Thinly slice the lemon or lime.
2 Wrap a lemon or lime slice round each prawn. Thread on to four wooden skewers, alternating with the cubes of monkfish or cod fillet and cucumber. Place the kebabs in a flameproof dish.
3 Spoon the vinaigrette and chopped dill over the kebabs. Grill for 4–5 minutes on each side, basting occasionally. Season with salt and pepper, and serve immediately on a bed of green salad. Garnish with a few dill sprigs, and serve with crusty bread.

NOT SUITABLE FOR FREEZING

130 Calories per serving

Haddock and Soured Cream Gratin

PREPARATION TIME: 5 minutes
COOKING TIME: 15 minutes

Serves 2

350 g (12 oz) frozen haddock fillet, thawed
butter
2 firm tomatoes, chopped
150 ml (5 fl oz) soured cream
15 ml (1 level tbsp) chopped fresh chives
15 ml (1 level tbsp) chopped fresh parsley
25 g (1 oz) Gruyère cheese, grated
salt and pepper

1 Skin the haddock if necessary and chop roughly. Choose a shallow, flameproof serving dish just large enough to take the fish in a single layer. Put a knob of butter in the dish and place under a hot grill to melt.
2 Add the fish and turn in the butter. Return to the grill for 10 minutes, turning occasionally, until cooked.
3 Mix the tomatoes with the soured cream, herbs, grated cheese and salt and pepper to taste. Spoon over the fish and cook under the grill until bubbling. Serve immediately.

NOT SUITABLE FOR FREEZING

380 Calories per serving

Horseradish Grilled Herring

PREPARATION TIME: 10 minutes
COOKING TIME: 10 minutes

SERVES 4

4 herring, about 200 g (7 oz) each
50 g (2 oz) walnut pieces, finely chopped
30 ml (2 level tbsp) creamed horseradish
15 ml (1 level tbsp) medium oatmeal
150 ml (5 fl oz) soured cream
5 ml (1 tsp) lemon juice
salt and pepper
oil for grilling

1 Cut the herring into 2.5 cm (1 inch) thick cutlets.
2 Mix the chopped walnuts with the horseradish, oatmeal, soured cream, lemon juice, and salt and pepper to taste.
3 Line the grill pan with foil. Brush the herring cutlets lightly with oil and grill for 2–3 minutes on each side or until almost cooked through.
4 Spread the horseradish mixture evenly over the top of the herring cutlets. Grill for a further 3–4 minutes or until golden brown. Serve immediately.

NOT SUITABLE FOR FREEZING

625 Calories per serving

Crisp-Fried Fish Nuggets with Garlic Dip

PREPARATION TIME: 20 minutes
COOKING TIME: 10 minutes

SERVES 4

450 g (1 lb) cod fillet
30 ml (2 level tbsp) plain flour
15 ml (1 level tbsp) paprika
1 large egg, beaten
120 ml (8 level tbsp) dried breadcrumbs
60 ml (4 level tbsp) sesame seeds
125 g (4 oz) onion, skinned and finely chopped
1 garlic clove, skinned and crushed
150 g (5 oz) natural yogurt
oil for frying

1 Skin the cod, if necessary, and cut into 2.5 cm (1 inch) pieces. Mix together the flour and paprika and stir in the fish. Dip in the beaten egg.
2 Mix together the breadcrumbs and sesame seeds. Toss the fish in this mixture, then chill for 10 minutes.
3 Stir together the onion, garlic and yogurt. Cover and chill.
4 Heat a little oil in a non-stick frying pan and sauté the fish for 3–4 minutes, a few pieces at a time. Drain well on absorbent kitchen paper. Serve with the dip and a mixed salad.

NOT SUITABLE FOR FREEZING

425 Calories per serving

FRESH TUNA NIÇOISE

PREPARATION TIME: 20 minutes
COOKING TIME: 8 minutes

SERVES 6

225 g (8 oz) cucumber
1 bunch of spring onions, trimmed
50 g (2 oz) pitted black olives
225 g (8 oz) cherry tomatoes, halved
450 g (1 lb) fine green beans
300 ml (½ pint) tomato juice
20 ml (4 tsp) balsamic vinegar
30 ml (2 tbsp) lemon juice
30 ml (2 tbsp) soy sauce
60 ml (4 tbsp) olive oil
30 ml (2 tbsp) runny honey
2 garlic cloves, skinned and crushed
salt and pepper
6 tuna steaks, about 175 g (6 oz) each
3 hard-boiled eggs, shelled and quartered

1 Cut the cucumber in half lengthways and remove the seeds. Slice into diagonal chunks. Slice the spring onions in half lengthways and cut into similar-sized pieces. Place both in a bowl with the olives and tomatoes.

2 Top, tail and halve the beans and plunge into boiling water for 3 minutes. Lift out with a slotted spoon and place in a bowl of ice cold water for a few minutes. Drain well. Mix with the other green vegetables, cover and chill in the refrigerator.

3 Whisk together the tomato juice, vinegar, lemon juice, soy sauce, olive oil and honey. Add the garlic and plenty of seasoning.

4 Dip the tuna steaks in the dressing, one by one, coating them on both sides. Place in the grill pan and cook under the grill for 4 minutes each side or until they are golden and feel firm to the touch.

5 Toss the vegetables in a little of the dressing and divide equally between six serving plates. Add the eggs. Top with a tuna steak. Serve extra dressing separately.

NOT SUITABLE FOR FREEZING

500 Calories per serving

VARIATION

Replace the tuna steaks with salmon fillets, which will only need grilling lightly, or use smoked trout or peppered mackerel fillets.

Fresh Tuna Niçoise

52

HOT AND SOUR FISH

PREPARATION TIME: 10 minutes
COOKING TIME: 8 minutes

SERVES 4

350 g (12 oz) skinless fresh haddock fillet
15 ml (1 tbsp) oil
5 ml (1 level tsp) ground turmeric
50 g (2 oz) onion, skinned and finely chopped
1 green chilli, deseeded and finely chopped
225 g (8 oz) courgettes, trimmed and thinly sliced
50 g (2 oz) frozen peas
10 ml (2 tsp) lemon juice
60 ml (4 level tbsp) hoisin sauce
150 ml (¼ pint) water
salt and pepper

1 Cut the haddock fillet into large bite-sized pieces.
2 Heat the oil in a large non-stick frying pan, add the turmeric, onion, chilli, courgettes and peas, and stir-fry over a high heat for 4–5 minutes or until the vegetables begin to soften.
3 Add the fish to the pan with the lemon juice, hoisin sauce and water. Bring to the boil, then reduce the heat and simmer, uncovered, for 2–3 minutes or until the fish is just tender. Season with salt and pepper, and serve immediately.

NOT SUITABLE FOR FREEZING

135 Calories per serving

GOLDEN-CRUMBED PLAICE

PREPARATION TIME: 10 minutes
COOKING TIME: 5–10 minutes

SERVES 4

450 g (1 lb) fillet of plaice, skinned
a dash of lemon juice
1 bay leaf
salt and pepper
40 g (1½ oz) butter or margarine
50 g (2 oz) fresh brown breadcrumbs
3 celery sticks, trimmed and roughly chopped
25 g (1 oz) chopped walnuts
30 ml (2 level tbsp) chopped fresh parsley
flat-leaf parsley, to garnish

1 If necessary, divide each fish fillet in half, then roll up with the skinned side inside. Secure with cocktail sticks.
2 Place the fish in a sauté pan, and barely cover with water. Add the lemon juice, bay leaf and salt and pepper to taste. Cover and simmer for about 5 minutes or until tender.
3 Meanwhile, melt the butter or margarine in a frying pan. Add the crumbs and fry, stirring occasionally, until beginning to brown. Mix in the celery and walnuts, and cook until the crumbs are golden. Stir in the parsley and seasoning.
4 Drain the fish on absorbent kitchen paper. Remove the cocktail sticks. Serve immediately, topped with the golden crumbs and garnished with flat-leaf parsley.

NOT SUITABLE FOR FREEZING

255 Calories per serving

*L*IGHT SEAFOOD SAUTÉ

PREPARATION TIME: 15 minutes

COOKING TIME: 15 minutes

SERVES 4

30 ml (2 tbsp) oil

450 g (1 lb) monkfish fillet, skinned and cut into bite-sized pieces

1 bunch of spring onions, sliced

1 garlic clove, skinned and finely chopped

2.5 cm (1 inch) piece of fresh root ginger, peeled and finely chopped

275 g (10 oz) leeks, trimmed and roughly sliced

1 red pepper, deseeded and roughly chopped

125 g (4 oz) cooked peeled prawns

15 ml (1 tbsp) each hoisin sauce, light soy sauce and dry sherry

black pepper

1 Heat the oil in a large non-stick frying pan, add the monkfish and sauté for 2–3 minutes. Remove from the pan, using a slotted spoon. Add the onions, garlic and ginger to the pan and sauté for 2 minutes or until beginning to soften. Add the leeks and red pepper, and sauté for a further 10 minutes or until softened, stirring constantly.

2 Return the monkfish to the pan with the prawns, hoisin sauce, soy sauce and the sherry. Season with plenty of black pepper (the soy sauce is fairly salty). Cook for a final 30 seconds–1 minute, stirring. Serve at once.

NOT SUITABLE FOR FREEZING

230 Calories per serving

*S*MOKED MACKEREL AND CUCUMBER STIR-FRY

PREPARATION TIME: 10 minutes

COOKING TIME: 5 minutes

Prepare all the ingredients before you start to cook. Plain smoked mackerel fillets can be used – add black pepper to taste.

SERVES 2

10 ml (2 level tsp) sesame seeds (optional)

175 g (6 oz) peppered smoked mackerel fillets

½ cucumber

1 bunch of spring onions (about 10)

15 ml (1 tbsp) oil

15 ml (1 tbsp) soy sauce

10 ml (2 tsp) lemon juice

crusty bread, to serve

1 Toast the sesame seeds, if using, under the grill. Set aside.

2 Skin the fish and slice diagonally into 2.5 cm (1 inch) strips. Cut the cucumber into thick strips about 5 cm (2 inches) in length. Trim and shred the spring onions.

3 Heat the oil in a large frying pan, add the cucumber and spring onions, and cook over a high heat for 2–3 minutes, stirring constantly.

4 Mix in the fish, and stir-fry carefully for a further 1 minute before adding the soy sauce and lemon juice. Allow to bubble up, sprinkle over the sesame seeds, if using, and serve immediately with crusty bread.

NOT SUITABLE FOR FREEZING

335 Calories per serving

THAI GRILLED CARAMELISED FISH

PREPARATION TIME: 25 minutes
COOKING TIME: 4–5 minutes

The traditional recipe requires whole fish, but fillets or steaks can be substituted.

SERVES 4

4 whole plaice fillets, skinned
5 ml (1 level tsp) salt
juice of 2 limes
60–90 ml (4–6 level tbsp) demerara sugar
lime wedges, to garnish

1 Halve each fillet, sprinkle with the salt and lime juice, and roll up. Set aside for 20–25 minutes. Just before grilling, rub the fish all over with sugar.
2 Grill the fish under a preheated grill for 4–5 minutes each side, or until cooked and caramelised. Serve immediately garnished with lime wedges.

NOT SUITABLE FOR FREEZING

220 Calories per serving

Thai Grilled Caramelised Fish

CREAMY FISH AND PUMPKIN PIE

PREPARATION TIME: 10 minutes
COOKING TIME: 20–25 minutes

SERVES 4

700 g (1½ lb) pumpkin or squash, peeled,
deseeded and roughly chopped
salt and pepper
350 g (12 oz) courgettes, roughly chopped
450 g (1 lb) cod fillet, skinned
100 ml (4 fl oz) skimmed milk
3 peppercorns
1 bay leaf
vegetable margarine
45 ml (3 level tbsp) plain flour
50 ml (2 fl oz) dry white wine
75 g (3 oz) low-fat soft cheese with garlic
and herbs
30 ml (2 level tbsp) chopped fresh tarragon or
5 ml (1 level tsp) dried
4 sheets of filo pastry, about 50 g (2 oz)
total weight
15 ml (1 level tbsp) sesame seeds

1 Cook the pumpkin in simmering salted water for 5 minutes. Add the courgettes and simmer for a further 5 minutes, or until just tender. Drain well.
2 Meanwhile, cut the cod into large chunks. Place in a pan with the milk, peppercorns, bay leaf and 100 ml (4 fl oz) water, and simmer for about 2 minutes or until just tender. Drain well, reserving the cooking liquor.
3 Melt 30 ml (2 level tbsp) margarine in a saucepan and blend in the flour. Cook, stirring, for 1–2 minutes, then remove from the heat and gradually add 275 ml (9 fl oz) reserved cooking liquor and the wine. Bring to the boil, stirring, until a smooth sauce is formed. Remove from the heat and add the cheese and tarragon. Season with salt and pepper.

4 Place the vegetables and fish in a 1.1 litre (2 pint) ovenproof dish. Spoon over the sauce. Crumple the pastry on top and brush with 15 ml (1 tbsp) melted low-fat spread. Sprinkle with sesame seeds.
5 Bake in the oven at 200°C (400°F) mark 6 for about 15 minutes or until golden brown and piping hot.

NOT SUITABLE FOR FREEZING

330 Calories per serving

PLAICE WITH PESTO

PREPARATION TIME: 15 minutes
COOKING TIME: 15 minutes

Pesto is a vivid green sauce, bursting with the flavour of basil, pine nuts and Parmesan. It can be bought in most supermarkets or delicatessens.

SERVES 4

8 small plaice fillets, about 550 g (1¼ lb)
total weight
3 spring onions
125 g (4 oz) fine asparagus or fine French beans
125 g (4 oz) mangetouts
125 g (4 oz) carrots, peeled
75 g (3 oz) oyster mushrooms, wiped
125 g (4 oz) whole baby sweetcorn
15 ml (1 level tbsp) pesto sauce
30 ml (2 tbsp) lemon juice
100 ml (4 fl oz) light stock
salt and pepper
30 ml (2 tbsp) vegetable oil

1 Skin the plaice fillets and divide each one along the natural centre line into two fillets. Roll up loosely (keeping the skin-side inside).
2 Trim the spring onions and asparagus and cut into 6.5 cm (2½ inch) lengths. Top and tail

the mangetouts and French beans, if using. Cut the carrots into thick 6.5 cm (2½ inch) sticks, trim the mushrooms and halve the sweetcorn cobs lengthways.

3 Place the fish, pesto sauce, lemon juice, stock and seasoning in a medium saucepan. Bring to the boil, then reduce the heat and cover tightly with damp greaseproof paper and the lid. Simmer gently for about 10 minutes or until the fish is cooked.

4 Meanwhile, steam the prepared vegetables until just tender, or heat some oil in a sauté pan and stir-fry for 3–4 minutes.

5 To serve, spoon the vegetables on to individual serving plates and top with the fish fillets and pan juices.

NOT SUITABLE FOR FREEZING

255 Calories per serving

---

*Q*UICK SPICED FISH

PREPARATION TIME: 10 minutes
COOKING TIME: 20 minutes

SERVES 4

15 ml (1 tbsp) olive oil
125 g (4 oz) onion, skinned and roughly chopped
350 g (12 oz) leeks, trimmed and sliced
7.5 ml (1½ level tsp) mild curry powder
175 g (6 oz) courgettes, sliced
125 g (4 oz) celery, trimmed and sliced
1.1 litres (2 pints) skimmed milk
1 fish stock cube
2 bay leaves
5 ml (1 level tsp) tomato purée
200 g (7 oz) can sweetcorn, drained
salt and pepper
10 ml (2 level tsp) cornflour

450 g (1 lb) cod fillet
15 ml (1 tbsp) sherry
15 ml (1 level tbsp) chopped fresh parsley
crusty granary bread, to serve

1 Heat the oil in a large saucepan, add the onion, leeks and curry powder, and sauté for 3–4 minutes or until softened. Add the courgettes and celery and cook for a further 2 minutes, stirring all the time.

2 Mix in the milk, crumble in the stock cube, and add the bay leaves, tomato purée and sweetcorn. Season with salt and pepper. Bring to the boil, then reduce the heat and simmer, stirring, for 5 minutes. Blend the cornflour to a smooth paste with a little cold water. Off the heat, stir the cornflour into the milk mixture. Bring to the boil, stirring, then simmer gently until thickened.

3 Meanwhile, skin the fish and cut into large cubes. Add to the pan and simmer gently for a further 5 minutes or until cooked through. Stir in the sherry and parsley before serving with crusty granary bread.

NOT SUITABLE FOR FREEZING

290 Calories per serving

Mussels with Spicy Coconut Broth

PREPARATION TIME: about 15 minutes
COOKING TIME: 15 minutes

SERVES 4

1.8 kg (4 lb) fresh mussels
30 ml (2 tbsp) vegetable oil
1 small onion, peeled and finely chopped
1–2 garlic cloves, finely chopped
2–3 dried red chillies, crumbled
15 ml (1 tbsp) ground coriander
2 lemon grass stalks
handful of fresh coriander leaves
5 cm (2 inch) piece of fresh or dried galangal
6 kaffir lime leaves
300 ml (½ pint) coconut milk
salt and pepper

1 Clean and thoroughly rinse the mussels, removing the 'beards'. Discard any mussels that refuse to close when tapped.
2 Heat the oil in a large saucepan, add the onion, garlic and chillies and sauté for about 5 minutes until the onion is softened. Add the ground coriander and cook, stirring, for 1 minute.
3 Cut each lemon grass stalk in half and bruise with a rolling pin. Roughly chop half of the coriander leaves. Thinly slice the galangal. Add these ingredients to the onion mixture with the lime leaves. Stir in the coconut milk and 150 ml (¼ pint) water. Bring to the boil, lower the heat and simmer gently for 10 minutes. Season carefully.
4 Add the mussels to the pan, then cover with a tight-fitting lid. Simmer gently for about 5 minutes until the mussels open. Discard any unopened ones.
5 Spoon the mussels into deep serving bowls and scatter with the reserved coriander.

NOT SUITABLE FOR FREEZING

405 Calories per serving

Steamed Mussels with Lemon Grass and Basil

PREPARATION TIME: 10 minutes
COOKING TIME: 5 minutes

Make sure all the mussels are tightly shut before cooking – if open, tap gently to see if they close.

SERVES 4

900 g (2 lb) fresh mussels
2 lemon grass stalks
7.5 cm (3 inch) piece of fresh root ginger, peeled and roughly chopped
10 sprigs of fresh basil
torn basil leaves, to garnish

1 Clean and thoroughly rinse the mussels, removing the 'beards'. Slice the lemon grass into 7.5 cm (3 inch) pieces and crush lightly.
2 Place all the ingredients in a large saucepan and add enough water to come 1 cm (½ inch) up the sides of the pan.
3 Bring to the boil, cover and steam over a moderate heat for about 5 minutes or until all the mussels have opened. Discard any that remain closed. Drain and serve, garnished with torn basil leaves.

NOT SUITABLE FOR FREEZING

150 Calories per serving

Steamed Mussels with Lemon Grass and Basil

SALMON WITH TOMATO VINAIGRETTE

PREPARATION TIME: 20 minutes
COOKING TIME: 15 minutes

SERVES 6

olive oil
15 ml (1 level tbsp) Dijon mustard
50 ml (2 fl oz) champagne vinegar or white wine vinegar
75 g (3 oz) shallots, skinned and chopped
2 garlic cloves, skinned and crushed
15 ml (1 level tbsp) caster sugar
550 g (1¼ lb) tomatoes, preferably plum
60 ml (4 level tbsp) chopped fresh chives
30 ml (2 level tbsp) chopped fresh tarragon
salt and pepper
six 200 g (7 oz) salmon fillets or steaks, skinned
fresh herbs and yellow tomatoes, to garnish

1 First, make a vinaigrette with 200 ml (7 fl oz) oil, the mustard, vinegar, shallots, garlic and sugar. Skin the tomatoes and dice the flesh, discarding the seeds. Add to the vinaigrette with the chives and tarragon. Season with salt and pepper.
2 Brush the salmon with oil and season. Grill for 10–15 minutes or until tender and well browned (salmon steaks take a little longer, and need more oil).
3 Place the fish on serving plates and half-cover with the vinaigrette. Garnish with fresh herbs and tomatoes.

NOT SUITABLE FOR FREEZING

690 Calories per serving

SALMON AND PESTO PARCELS

PREPARATION TIME: 10 minutes
COOKING TIME: 15 minutes

SERVES 2

10 ml (2 level tsp) pesto sauce
75 ml (5 level tbsp) fromage frais or low-fat soft cheese
two 30.5 × 45.5 cm (12 × 18 inch) sheets of filo pastry, about 50 g (2 oz) total weight
25 g (1 oz) butter, melted
two 125 g (4 oz) salmon fillets, skinned
50 g (2 oz) button mushrooms, wiped and sliced
salt and pepper
salad leaves, tarragon and sliced beetroot, to serve (optional)

1 Mix the pesto sauce with the fromage frais or low-fat soft cheese.
2 Halve each sheet of filo pastry. Layer two pieces of the filo, and butter lightly between and on top of the pastry layers.
3 Place the salmon fillets in the centre of the pastry. Top with the mushrooms and half of the pesto sauce mixture, and season with salt and pepper. Wrap the pastry around to enclose the fish, using the remaining butter to brush over the parcels. Place the parcels on a baking sheet lightly brushed with butter.
4 Bake in the oven at 200°C (400°F) mark 6 for about 15 minutes or until well browned. To serve, open the pastry and spoon in the remaining pesto sauce mixture. Serve accompanied by salad leaves, tarragon and sliced beetroot, if liked.

NOT SUITABLE FOR FREEZING

410 Calories per serving

Salmon and Thyme Butter Parcels

PREPARATION TIME: 20 minutes
COOKING TIME: 10 minutes

Boning out the cutlets produces an attractive shape, but it's not essential.

SERVES 2

2 salmon cutlets, 150 g (5 oz) each
15 ml (1 tbsp) oil
25 g (1 oz) butter, softened
1 garlic clove, skinned and crushed
5 ml (1 level tsp) mustard seeds
15 ml (1 level tbsp) chopped fresh thyme or 5 ml (1 level tsp) dried
salt and pepper
2 tomatoes, skinned, deseeded and roughly chopped
fresh thyme, to garnish

1 Carefully remove the centre bone from each cutlet. Curl each half cutlet around to form a medallion and tie with fine string.
2 Heat the oil in a sauté pan, add the salmon and cook until browned on both sides. Drain on absorbent kitchen paper and cool.
3 Blend together the butter, garlic, mustard seeds, thyme and salt and pepper to taste.
4 Cut four pieces of greaseproof paper, about 25.5 cm (10 inches) square. Place a salmon medallion in the centre of each and top with the herb butter and tomato. Wrap the paper over and tie with string to form bundles.
5 Bake in the oven at 200°C (400°F) mark 6 for 10 minutes or until the salmon is cooked through. Garnish with fresh thyme and serve.

NOT SUITABLE FOR FREEZING

350 Calories per serving

Grilled Lemon Sole with Salsa Verde

PREPARATION TIME: 15 minutes
COOKING TIME: 10 minutes

'Salsa verde' means green sauce. Made with basil leaves, it is delicious served with any white fish.

SERVES 6

2 bunches of fresh basil, about 2 large handfuls, chopped
2 garlic cloves, skinned and crushed
125 g (4 oz) Parmesan cheese, freshly grated
4 hard-boiled eggs, chopped
olive oil
salt and pepper
12 lemon sole fillets, skinned
flat-leaf parsley, to garnish

1 Mix the basil with the garlic, Parmesan and hard-boiled eggs. Add enough oil to make a moist mixture for the salsa that will be stiff enough to form into lozenge shapes (see below). Season to taste with salt and pepper.
2 Spread each sole fillet out on a board, lightly flatten with the side of a knife, then fold each one in half. Season with salt and pepper, brush with oil and grill for 8–10 minutes or until cooked, turning the fillets once during cooking.
3 To complete, lay two of the fillets on each of six individual warmed serving plates. With two spoons, make lozenge shapes with the salsa verde and arrange beside the fish. Garnish with sprigs of flat-leaf parsley.

NOT SUITABLE FOR FREEZING

400 Calories per serving

Salmon and Pesto Parcels (page 62)   *Opposite: Grilled Lemon Sole with Salsa Verde (page 63)*

*M*ONKFISH IN TOMATO SAUCE

PREPARATION TIME: 10 minutes
COOKING TIME: 20 minutes

SERVES 4

700 g (1½ lb) monkfish fillet
oil
1 garlic clove, skinned and chopped, or 2.5 ml
(½ level tsp) garlic purée
125 g (4 oz) onion, skinned and finely chopped
15 ml (1 level tbsp) plain flour
150 ml (¼ pint) white wine
400 g (14 oz) can chopped tomatoes
10 ml (2 tsp) lemon juice
salt and pepper
2.5 ml (½ level tsp) sugar
5 ml (1 level tsp) dried dill weed
chopped fresh parsley, to garnish
boiled white rice and salad, to serve

1 Cut the fish into bite-sized chunks, discarding the skin. Heat a little oil in a flameproof casserole, add the fish, garlic and onion, and sauté quickly. Stir in the flour and gradually pour in the wine with 75 ml (3 fl oz) water.

2 Add the remaining ingredients and bring to the boil. Cover and cook in the oven at 190°C (375°F) mark 5 for 20 minutes, or until the fish is cooked.

3 Adjust the seasoning, garnish with a little chopped parsley and serve with rice and a crisp salad.

NOT SUITABLE FOR FREEZING

250 Calories per serving

VARIATION

Use cod fillet instead of monkfish but make sure the chunks remain whole.

VEGETARIAN VERVE

QUORN KEBABS WITH TOMATO SALSA

PREPARATION TIME: 20 minutes
COOKING TIME: 6 minutes

Quorn is a vegetable protein which is sold ready diced. Look out for it in the chilled cabinets of supermarkets.

SERVES 4

15 ml (1 level tbsp) Cajun seasoning
5 ml (1 level tsp) mild chilli seasoning
30 ml (2 tbsp) Ginger and Orange Sauce
grated rind and juice of 2 limes
45 ml (3 tbsp) olive oil
350 g (12 oz) quorn
1 large tomato, finely diced
1 small red pepper, deseeded and finely diced
1 very small red chilli, deseeded and finely diced
3 spring onions, trimmed and sliced
¼ small cucumber, finely diced
30 ml (2 level tbsp) chopped fresh parsley
15 ml (1 tbsp) olive oil
salt and pepper
2 frozen corn cobs, about 200 g (7 oz) each, thawed

lime wedges, chopped chilli and parsley sprigs, to garnish (optional)
natural yogurt, to serve (optional)

1 Mix the Cajun seasoning, chilli seasoning and Ginger and Orange Sauce together in a glass bowl. Add the lime rind and juice and 30 ml (2 tbsp) olive oil. Stir in the quorn cubes and leave to marinate for at least 15 minutes.

2 Meanwhile, mix together the tomato, red pepper, chilli, onions, cucumber, parsley, remaining oil and seasoning.

3 Cut the corn cobs into thin slices and thread on to fine skewers with the quorn cubes (taking care that the quorn does not break up). Brush the kebabs with the remaining marinade and grill for about 6 minutes, turning and basting occasionally, until the quorn is heated through and the corn is evenly charred. Serve with the salsa garnished with lime, chopped chilli and parsley, and accompanied by natural yogurt, if wished.

NOT SUITABLE FOR FREEZING

340 Calories per serving

ROASTED PEPPERS WITH GOAT'S CHEESE AND LENTILS

PREPARATION TIME: 10 minutes
COOKING TIME: 20 minutes

SERVES 2

125 g (4 oz) red lentils
salt and pepper
2 red peppers, about 175 g (6 oz) each, halved and deseeded
25 g (1 oz) butter or margarine
125 g (4 oz) onion, skinned and finely chopped
75 g (3 oz) celery, skinned and finely chopped
75 g (3 oz) soft fresh goat's cheese or low-fat soft cheese
1 egg
about 8 pitted black olives, roughly chopped
fresh basil, to garnish

1 Cook the lentils in about 300 ml (½ pint) boiling salted water for 12–15 minutes or until just tender. Drain.
2 Meanwhile, place the pepper halves under a hot grill for 10–12 minutes, turning occasionally. The skin will brown and the flesh soften.
3 Melt the butter or margarine in a sauté pan, add the onion and celery and sauté for 2–3 minutes. Stir in the lentils. Off the heat, beat in the cheese, egg, olives and seasoning. Divide among the pepper halves.
4 Grill the peppers for 2–3 minutes or until golden. Garnish with fresh basil and serve.

NOT SUITABLE FOR FREEZING

475 Calories per serving

CHILLI BEANS

PREPARATION TIME: 5 minutes
COOKING TIME: 25 minutes

Any type of canned beans or pulses can be used in this recipe.

SERVES 2–3

30 ml (2 tbsp) oil
125 g (4 oz) onion, skinned and roughly chopped
2.5 ml (½ level tsp) chilli powder
400 g (14 oz) can chopped tomatoes
300 ml (½ pint) vegetable stock
5 ml (1 level tsp) English mustard powder
15 ml (1 level tbsp) black treacle
400 g (14 oz) can butter beans, drained and rinsed
440 g (15½ oz) can chick peas, drained and rinsed
salt and pepper
15 ml (1 level tbsp) chopped fresh coriander
pasta, rice or garlic bread, to serve

1 Heat the oil in a medium saucepan, add the onion and chilli powder and cook gently until the onion begins to soften and brown.
2 Add all the remaining ingredients, except the coriander, and simmer, uncovered, for about 20 minutes.
3 Stir in the coriander, adjust the seasoning and serve hot with pasta, rice or garlic bread.

NOT SUITABLE FOR FREEZING

635 Calories per serving for 2
425 Calories per serving for 3

Roasted Peppers with Goat's Cheese and Lentils

Winter Vegetables with Lentils and Ginger

PREPARATION TIME: 15 minutes
COOKING TIME: 16 minutes

SERVES 4

45 ml (3 tbsp) olive oil
5 ml (1 level tsp) ground cumin
15 ml (1 level tbsp) ground coriander
15 ml (1 level tbsp) mustard powder
1 garlic clove, skinned and crushed
1 cm (½ inch) piece of fresh root ginger, peeled and chopped
225 g (8 oz) frozen baby onions
225 g (8 oz) button mushrooms, wiped and halved if necessary
225 g (8 oz) carrots, peeled and thinly sliced
225 g (8 oz) trimmed leeks, thickly sliced
275 g (10 oz) parsnips, peeled and diced
175 g (6 oz) split red lentils
900 ml (1½ pints) vegetable stock
chopped fresh coriander, to finish
salt and pepper

1 Heat the oil in a large saucepan, add the spices, and sauté, stirring, for 1 minute. Mix in the remaining ingredients, except the coriander.
2 Bring to the boil, then reduce the heat, cover and simmer for 15 minutes or until the lentils are just tender. Before serving, stir in the coriander and adjust the seasoning.

NOT SUITABLE FOR FREEZING

290 Calories per serving

Vegetable Couscous

PREPARATION TIME: 10 minutes
COOKING TIME: 15 minutes

Look out for quick-cook couscous, which only needs to be moistened slightly and steamed for 2 minutes. If your supermarket doesn't stock couscous, use bulgar wheat, soaked and steamed as below, or serve the vegetables with plain, boiled rice.

SERVES 4

225 g (8 oz) quick-cook couscous
15 ml (1 tbsp) oil
2 garlic cloves, skinned and crushed
10 ml (2 level tsp) ground cumin
2.5 ml (½ level tsp) mild chilli seasoning
2.5 ml (½ level tsp) ground ginger
60 ml (4 level tbsp) tomato purée
1 bay leaf
1 vegetable stock cube
225 g (8 oz) aubergine, cut into large chunks
175 g (6 oz) carrots, peeled and cut into large chunks
175 g (6 oz) onion, skinned and chopped
175 g (6 oz) courgettes, cut into large chunks
175 g (6 oz) frozen broad beans, thawed, or canned chick peas, drained
salt and pepper
750 ml (1¼ pints) water
mild chilli seasoning and fresh herbs, to garnish (optional)

1 Place the couscous on a tray and soak according to the manufacturer's instructions.
2 Heat the oil in a medium saucepan (over which a metal sieve or colander will fit), add the garlic and spices, and cook gently for 1 minute, stirring occasionally. Stir in the tomato purée and bay leaf and crumble in the vegetable stock cube.
3 Add the vegetables and broad beans or chick peas to the pan with the seasoning. Pour in the water, cover and bring to the boil.

Uncover the pan and boil the vegetables rapidly for 8 minutes.

4 Meanwhile, fork the couscous to break up any lumps and spread in a metal sieve or colander lined with a clean J-cloth or muslin. Place over the cooking vegetables, cover and cook for a further 5 minutes or until the vegetables are tender, the sauce well reduced and the couscous piping hot. Adjust the seasoning of the vegetables.

5 Spoon the couscous on to a serving dish and pile the vegetables and juices on top. Sprinkle with chilli seasoning and garnish with fresh herbs, if wished.

NOT SUITABLE FOR FREEZING

260 Calories per serving

❧

MUSHROOM, LEEK AND FETA TARTS

PREPARATION TIME: 10 minutes
COOKING TIME: 15 minutes

These tartlets are as light as air, with a substantial filling – they're good as a snack lunch or starter.

SERVES 4

45 ml (3 level tbsp) butter or margarine
12 pieces of filo pastry, each 12.5 cm (5 inches) square
30 ml (2 tbsp) olive or sunflower oil
225 g (8 oz) leeks, trimmed and finely sliced
350 g (12 oz) mixed mushrooms, such as button, oyster, flat, etc., wiped and sliced
90 ml (6 tbsp) vegetable stock
15 ml (1 level tbsp) chopped fresh tarragon
175 g (6 oz) feta cheese, crumbled or grated
salt and pepper

1 Melt the butter or margarine in a saucepan. Brush four 10 cm (4 inch) tart tins or similar-sized Yorkshire pudding tins with the fat. Layer the pastry squares in the tins, brushing between each layer and moving each pastry square round a quarter of a turn. Press well into the corners of the tins. Brush with the remaining fat. The tarts should have a frilly, tattered edge. Bake in the oven at 200°C (400°F) mark 6 for 8–10 minutes or until golden. Cool slightly and remove from the tins.

2 Meanwhile, heat the oil in a saucepan, add the leeks, cover and cook over a gentle heat for 5 minutes or until beginning to soften.

3 Add the mushrooms, stir and pour in the stock. Cover and cook gently for another 5 minutes. Uncover and boil rapidly until almost all the liquid has evaporated. Stir in the tarragon and feta cheese.

4 Season to taste and spoon evenly into the tartlets. Serve immediately.

NOT SUITABLE FOR FREEZING

385 Calories per serving

❧

Overleaf: From left to right: Mushroom, Leek and Feta Tarts; Quorn Kebabs with Tomato Salsa (page 67); Vegetable Couscous

Mushroom Fricassee with Couscous

PREPARATION TIME: 5 minutes
COOKING TIME: 10 minutes

SERVES 2

150 ml (¼ pint) boiling water
125 g (4 oz) couscous
grated rind and juice of 1 lemon
salt and pepper
225–275 g (8–10 oz) flat or cup mushrooms
75 g (3 oz) butter or polyunsaturated margarine
10 ml (2 level tsp) plain flour
about 150 ml (¼ pint) milk
10 ml (2 level tsp) Dijon mustard
25 g (1 oz) pine nuts

1 Pour the boiling water over the couscous. Add the lemon rind, season with salt and pepper, and soak for about 5 minutes, stirring occasionally.
2 Slice the mushrooms into medium-sized pieces. Heat 50 g (2 oz) butter or margarine in a frying pan and quickly fry the mushrooms until just beginning to soften.
3 Stir in the flour and 150 ml (¼ pint) milk and bring to the boil. Bubble for 1–2 minutes, adding a little more milk if necessary. Remove from the heat and stir in the mustard and 10 ml (2 tsp) lemon juice. Adjust the seasoning.
4 Meanwhile, heat the remaining butter in a separate frying pan. Add the pine nuts and couscous, and cook over a high heat, stirring occasionally, until piping hot. Adjust the seasoning and serve with the mushrooms.

NOT SUITABLE FOR FREEZING

585 Calories per serving

Leek and Lentil Pilaff

PREPARATION TIME: 5 minutes
COOKING TIME: 25 minutes

Some types of rice are more absorbent than others, so add stock accordingly.

SERVES 4

450 g (1 lb) trimmed leeks
polyunsaturated oil
125 g (4 oz) blanched split almonds
10 ml (2 level tsp) ground coriander
175 g (6 oz) long-grain white rice
125 g (4 oz) split red lentils
750–900 ml (1¼–1½ pints) vegetable stock
1 garlic clove, skinned and crushed
salt and pepper

1 Split the leeks and divide into 2.5 cm (1 inch) lengths. Rinse and drain.
2 Heat a little oil in a medium-sized flame-proof casserole, add the leeks and almonds and cook until browned. Add the coriander and cook for 1 minute.
3 Stir in the rice, lentils, stock, garlic and seasoning. Bring to the boil.
4 Cover and simmer for 15–20 minutes, or until the rice and lentils are tender and most of the stock has been absorbed. Adjust the seasoning.

NOT SUITABLE FOR FREEZING

535 Calories per serving

SPINACH AND MUSHROOM OMELETTE

PREPARATION TIME: 5 minutes

COOKING TIME: 7 minutes

Meat-eaters could sauté chopped bacon with the mushrooms.

SERVES 2

225 g (8 oz) frozen chopped spinach, thawed
4 eggs
1.25 ml (¼ level tsp) freshly grated nutmeg
salt and pepper
40 g (1½ oz) butter or margarine
125 g (4 oz) button mushrooms, wiped and sliced
10 ml (2 level tsp) wholegrain mustard
142 ml (5 fl oz) carton soured cream

1 Press the spinach in a sieve or colander to remove excess liquid. Place in a blender with the eggs, nutmeg and seasoning, and blend until smooth.
2 Heat 25 g (1 oz) butter or margarine in a large, non-stick frying pan. When foaming, add the spinach mixture and cook until the base sets. Cook the top under a hot grill for 1–2 minutes. Cover with foil to keep warm.
3 Melt the remaining butter in a small pan, add the mushrooms and mustard and sauté until soft. Add the soured cream and seasoning and bring to the boil.
4 Spoon the mushrooms on one half of the omelette, then flip over the other half to enclose the mixture. Serve straight away, cut into wedges.

NOT SUITABLE FOR FREEZING

505 Calories per serving

OMELETTE WEDGES

PREPARATION TIME: 5 minutes

COOKING TIME: 15 minutes

Quicker to make than individual omelettes, these can be cut into wedges to serve.

SERVES 4

6 eggs
salt and pepper
25 g (1 oz) mature hard cheese, such as
Cheddar or Gouda, finely grated
15 ml (1 tbsp) oil, preferably olive
25 g (1 oz) butter
50 g (2 oz) garlic sausage, sliced into strips
125 g (4 oz) mozzarella cheese, sliced into strips
1 tomato, sliced into strips
bread, preferably crusty, to serve

1 Whisk the eggs with the seasoning, and stir in the grated hard cheese.
2 Heat the oil in a large, heavy, non-stick frying pan, add the butter and, when foaming, pour in the egg and cheese mixture. Cook gently for 5–6 minutes or until the mixture begins to set underneath.
3 Scatter the sausage, mozzarella and tomato over the top. Season again and continue to cook for 2–3 minutes or until the eggs are just set.
4 Place the pan under a preheated grill and cook the omelette until golden and completely set. Serve accompanied by crusty bread.

NOT SUITABLE FOR FREEZING

370 Calories per serving

Mixed Vegetable and Egg Supper

PREPARATION TIME: 20 minutes
COOKING TIME: 10 minutes

Serves 4

30 ml (2 tbsp) olive oil
350 g (12 oz) courgettes, sliced
1 medium green pepper, deseeded and roughly chopped
125 g (4 oz) onion, skinned and sliced
1 garlic clove, skinned and crushed
salt and pepper
10 ml (2 level tsp) chopped fresh rosemary or 2.5 ml (½ level tsp) dried
400 g (14 oz) can chopped tomatoes
4 eggs
50 g (2 oz) Cheddar or Gruyère cheese, grated
crusty bread, to serve

1 Heat the oil in a large sauté pan. Add the courgettes, pepper and onion and cook until beginning to soften and brown, stirring occasionally.
2 Stir in the garlic, seasoning, rosemary and tomatoes. Simmer, uncovered, until the vegetables are tender and the liquid has been well reduced.
3 Make four slight hollows in the vegetable mixture and break an egg carefully into each. Season the eggs with salt and plenty of pepper and top with the cheese.
4 Cook under a preheated grill for about 10 minutes (depending on how well done you like your eggs). Protect the pan handle with foil, if necessary.

NOT SUITABLE FOR FREEZING

280 Calories per serving

Spinach and Feta Puffs

PREPARATION TIME: 15 minutes
COOKING TIME: 15 minutes

Crisp, golden pasties – much simpler to make than they look.

Serves 4

25 g (1 oz) butter
50 g (2 oz) onion, skinned and finely chopped
125 g (4 oz) ready-prepared fresh spinach, or 75 g (3 oz) frozen leaf spinach, thawed
freshly grated nutmeg
black pepper
two 20.5 cm (8 inch) individual ready-rolled squares of puff pastry, thawed
50–75 g (2–3 oz) feta cheese, sliced
egg or milk, to glaze
mixed salad, to serve

1 Melt the butter in a medium-sized saucepan, add the onion and sauté for 2 minutes or until softened. Add the spinach with plenty of nutmeg and cook for a further 3–4 minutes (2 minutes if using frozen spinach), stirring until soft and the juices have evaporated. Season and cool slightly.
2 Cut each pastry square in half diagonally. Divide the spinach mixture between each triangle. Top with feta cheese. Dampen the edges of the pastry, fold over and seal well. Brush with egg or milk, to glaze.
3 Place on a baking sheet and cook in the oven at 200°C (400°F) mark 6 for about 15 minutes or until cooked through and golden brown. Serve immediately with a mixed salad.

NOT SUITABLE FOR FREEZING

330 Calories per serving

*R*ICOTTA AND SPINACH GNOCCHI

PREPARATION TIME: 10 minutes
COOKING TIME: 20 minutes

If you've ever had gnocchi in a restaurant, you'll know how rich they can be! This recipe uses ricotta cheese and a low-fat sauce, so these are much lighter.

SERVES 4

15 g (½ oz) low-fat spread
plain flour
450 ml (¾ pint) skimmed milk
90 g (3½ oz) Parmesan cheese, freshly grated
400 g (14 oz) fresh spinach or 225 g (8 oz) frozen chopped spinach, thawed
150 g (5 oz) ricotta cheese
1 egg yolk
salt and pepper
freshly grated nutmeg

1 Melt the low-fat spread in a pan, stir in 15 g (½ oz) flour and cook over a gentle heat for 1 minute. Off the heat, gradually stir in the milk. Bring to the boil, stirring, until it thickens. Simmer for 1–2 minutes, then stir in 25 g (1 oz) Parmesan. Keep warm.
2 Cook freshly washed spinach over a low heat for 1 minute. Drain, chop, and beat into the ricotta, with 50 g (2 oz) flour, the egg yolk and 50 g (2 oz) Parmesan, then season to taste.
3 Dust your hands with flour and shape heaped teaspoons of the mixture into rounds. Drop the rounds into simmering salted water. The gnocchi are cooked when they float to the surface, after 3–4 minutes. Lift out, drain and place in a lightly greased flameproof dish.
4 Spoon over the sauce and sprinkle with the remaining Parmesan. Grill until golden.

NOT SUITABLE FOR FREEZING

300 Calories per serving

*M*USHROOM AND PARMESAN RISOTTO

PREPARATION TIME: 10–15 minutes
COOKING TIME: 20 minutes

SERVES 4

1 lemon
225 g (8 oz) broccoli florets, broken into small sprigs
175 g (6 oz) French beans, topped and tailed, and cut in half lengthways
salt and pepper
30 ml (2 tbsp) olive oil
125 g (4 oz) onion, skinned and finely chopped
350 g (12 oz) Arborio (risotto) or long-grain white rice
a pinch of saffron threads (optional)
60 ml (4 tbsp) dry white wine
750 ml (1¼ pints) vegetable stock
175 g (6 oz) flat mushrooms, wiped and sliced
freshly grated Parmesan cheese, to serve

1 Pare the lemon rind and squeeze the juice.
2 Blanch the broccoli and beans together in boiling salted water for about 4 minutes. Drain and refresh under cold running water.
3 Heat the oil in a flameproof casserole and cook the onion for 2–3 minutes or until beginning to soften. Stir in the rice and saffron, if using, season well and add the wine, pared lemon rind, 30 ml (2 tbsp) lemon juice and the stock. Bring to the boil, stirring, then cover.
4 Simmer the risotto for 5 minutes. Stir in the mushrooms, broccoli and French beans. Re-cover and simmer for a further 5 minutes, or until the rice is almost tender and most of the liquid has been absorbed. Remove the lemon rind and serve with grated Parmesan.

NOT SUITABLE FOR FREEZING

420 Calories per serving

*P*ASTA PRONTO

*C*HICKEN LIVER BOLOGNAISE

PREPARATION TIME: 5–10 minutes
COOKING TIME: 25 minutes

Chicken livers produce a delicious, rich-flavoured sauce.

SERVES 4

30 ml (2 tbsp) olive oil

225 g (8 oz) onion, skinned and finely chopped

125 g (4 oz) carrot, peeled and finely chopped

1 celery stick, trimmed and finely chopped

175 g (6 oz) brown-cap mushrooms, wiped and sliced

125 g (4 oz) streaky bacon, derinded and snipped into small pieces

450 g (1 lb) chicken livers, trimmed and roughly chopped

2 garlic cloves, skinned and crushed

45 ml (3 level tbsp) tomato purée

150 ml (¼ pint) red wine

150 ml (¼ pint) beef stock

5 ml (1 level tsp) chopped fresh oregano or 2.5 ml (½ level tsp) dried

1 bay leaf

salt and pepper

350 g (12 oz) spaghetti or tagliatelle

1 Heat the oil in a large frying pan and cook the onion, carrot and celery until beginning to soften. Add the mushrooms and continue to cook, stirring, for a further 2–3 minutes.

2 Add the bacon, chicken livers and garlic to the pan and cook over a high heat, stirring occasionally, until the liver is beginning to brown.

3 Stir in the tomato purée, red wine, stock, herbs and seasoning. Bring to the boil, then simmer, covered, for about 20 minutes or until the sauce is a good rich colour.

4 Meanwhile, cook the pasta in boiling salted water until just tender. Drain well and put in a heated serving dish.

5 Adjust the seasoning of the sauce and pour over the hot pasta. Serve at once.

THE SAUCE CAN BE FROZEN AT THE END OF STEP 3

400 Calories per serving

Spaghetti with Chicken, Soured Cream and Gruyère Sauce

PREPARATION TIME: 5 minutes

COOKING TIME: 10 minutes

A great sauce to make with a few leftovers – chicken, wine and cheese. We've used Gruyère but any strong cheese will do.

Serves 2

125–175 g (4–6 oz) spaghetti
salt and pepper
grated rind of 1 lemon
100 ml (4 fl oz) dry white wine
225 g (8 oz) cooked chicken meat, skinned and roughly chopped
142 ml (5 fl oz) carton of soured cream
freshly grated nutmeg
60 ml (4 level tbsp) chopped fresh parsley
125 g (4 oz) Gruyère cheese, coarsely grated

1 Cook the spaghetti in boiling salted water until just tender.

2 Meanwhile, place the grated lemon rind and wine in a medium saucepan and simmer together for 2 minutes.

3 Add the chicken to the pan with all the remaining ingredients, except the cheese. Simmer gently for 2–3 minutes.

4 Remove from the heat and stir in the cheese. Season with salt and pepper.

5 Drain the spaghetti and put in a heated serving bowl. Pour over the sauce and serve at once.

NOT SUITABLE FOR FREEZING

590 Calories per serving

Golden Pasta Bake

PREPARATION TIME: 15 minutes

COOKING TIME: 15–20 minutes

Serves 8

30 ml (2 tbsp) oil
225 g (8 oz) button mushrooms, wiped and sliced
1 green pepper, deseeded and chopped
three 300 g (10.6 oz) cans Bolognaise sauce
225 g (8 oz) dried spaghetti or 350 g (12 oz) fresh
salt and pepper
50 g (2 oz) butter or margarine
50 g (2 oz) plain flour
568 ml (1 pint) milk
225 g (8 oz) Cheddar cheese, grated
parsley, to garnish (optional)

1 Heat the oil in a frying pan, add the mushrooms and green pepper, and sauté for 2 minutes. Add the Bolognaise sauce, bring to the boil, then reduce the heat and simmer for 5 minutes.

2 Meanwhile, cook the spaghetti in boiling salted water until just tender. Place the butter or margarine, flour and milk in a saucepan. Whisk over a low heat until the mixture thickens, then simmer for 1 minute. Remove from the heat, stir in three-quarters of the cheese and season.

3 Place the Bolognaise in the base of a 2.3 litre (4 pint) shallow ovenproof dish. Drain the spaghetti well, tip it into the ovenproof dish, and top with the cheese sauce. Sprinkle over the remaining cheese.

4 Bake in the oven at 200°C (400°F) mark 6 for 15–20 minutes or until golden brown. Garnish with parsley, if wished.

NOT SUITABLE FOR FREEZING

515 Calories per serving

Spring Vegetable Pasta

PREPARATION TIME: 10 minutes
COOKING TIME: 15 minutes

SERVES 4

125 g (4 oz) fresh asparagus or French beans, trimmed and cut into 5 cm (2 inch) lengths

225 g (8 oz) leeks, trimmed and thinly sliced diagonally

salt and pepper

175 g (6 oz) creamy chèvre (goat's cheese) or a full-fat soft cheese with garlic and herbs

150 g (5 oz) mascarpone cheese or 150 ml (5 fl oz) extra-thick double cream

50 g (2 oz) butter or margarine

30 ml (2 tbsp) olive oil

125 g (4 oz) onion, skinned and finely chopped

125 g (4 oz) carrot, peeled and thinly sliced diagonally

225 g (8 oz) brown cap mushrooms, wiped and thinly sliced

100 ml (4 fl oz) dry white wine

350 g (12 oz) crème fraîche

60 ml (4 level tbsp) chopped fresh herbs, such as parsley, thyme or sage

125 g (4 oz) petits pois

350 g (12 oz) penne

mascarpone, to garnish

1 Briefly blanch the asparagus or beans and leeks in boiling salted water for 3–4 minutes. Drain thoroughly. Mix together the chèvre and mascarpone or cream.

2 Heat the butter or margarine and the oil together in a large sauté pan. Stir in the onion and cook, stirring, for 3–4 minutes. Add the carrot and mushrooms and continue to cook for 2–3 minutes or until beginning to soften.

3 Stir in the wine, crème fraîche, herbs and peas, together with the blanched vegetables,

Spring Vegetable Pasta

and simmer very gently until thickened to a good coating consistency.

4 Meanwhile, cook the penne in boiling salted water until just tender.

5 Remove the sauce from the heat and gently stir in the cheese mixture until thoroughly mixed. Season to taste. Spoon on to the hot drained penne and serve immediately, garnished with a spoonful of mascarpone.

NOT SUITABLE FOR FREEZING

760 Calories per serving

Spaghetti with Toasted Garlic Crumbs

PREPARATION TIME: 10 minutes
COOKING TIME: 15 minutes

SERVES 4

25 ml (1 fl oz) olive oil

2 garlic cloves, skinned and crushed

75 g (3 oz) fine fresh white breadcrumbs

salt and pepper

45 ml (3 level tbsp) chopped fresh chives or parsley

350 g (12 oz) mixed egg and spinach spaghetti or linguini

1 Heat the oil in a large sauté pan and add the garlic and breadcrumbs. Stir the breadcrumbs over a medium heat for 3–4 minutes or until golden brown. Add a little more oil if necessary. Season and stir in the chopped herbs.

2 Cook the pasta in boiling salted water until just tender. Drain and toss with the breadcrumb mixture.

NOT SUITABLE FOR FREEZING

350 Calories per serving

Spaghetti with Pesto, Shallots and Olives

PREPARATION TIME: 10 minutes
COOKING TIME: 12 minutes

For a complete meal, serve this pasta dish with simple beef patties. Sauté 125 g (4 oz) chopped onion, then mix with 450 g (1 lb) lean minced beef, 45 ml (3 level tbsp) chopped fresh parsley and seasoning. Shape into 12 small patties and fry in olive oil for 5 minutes on each side. Top each with a slice of mozzarella and a cross of anchovy fillets. Brown under a hot grill for 1 minute (200 Calories per patty).

SERVES 4

175 g (6 oz) spaghetti
salt and pepper
25 g (1 oz) butter
olive oil
225 g (8 oz) shallots or small onions, skinned and thinly sliced
50 g (2 oz) pitted black olives
30 ml (2 level tbsp) pesto sauce
chopped fresh basil, to garnish

1 Cook the spaghetti in boiling salted water until just tender. Drain well.
2 Meanwhile, heat the butter with 30 ml (2 tbsp) oil in a sauté pan. Add the shallots or onions and cook gently, stirring occasionally, for 10–15 minutes or until soft and golden.
3 Stir in the black olives and pesto sauce, warm through and adjust the seasoning.
4 Toss the spaghetti with the shallot mixture and serve immediately, garnished with basil.

NOT SUITABLE FOR FREEZING

320 Calories per serving

Spaghetti with Pesto, Shallots and Olives served with simple beef patties (see above)

Sun-dried Tomato Pasta

PREPARATION TIME: 5 minutes
COOKING TIME: 25 minutes

SERVES 4

15 ml (1 tbsp) olive oil
75 g (3 oz) onion, skinned and roughly chopped
75 g (3 oz) carrots, peeled and roughly chopped
75 g (3 oz) celery, trimmed and roughly chopped
1 garlic clove, skinned and crushed
two 400 g (14 oz) cans chopped tomatoes
125 g (4 oz) sun-dried tomatoes in olive oil, drained and finely chopped
150 ml (¼ pint) light stock
100 ml (4 fl oz) dry white wine
salt and pepper
225 g (8 oz) dried, broad pasta noodles (pappardelle) or spaghetti
shavings of pecorino or Parmesan cheese, to serve

1 Heat the oil in a large saucepan, add the onion, carrot, celery and garlic, and cook, stirring, for about 5 minutes, or until they start to soften.
2 Stir in the canned tomatoes, sun-dried tomatoes, stock, wine and seasoning. Cover and simmer for about 20 minutes, stirring occasionally.
3 Blend half the sauce in a food processor, then return it to the pan, stirring in the remaining sauce.
4 Cook the pasta in boiling salted water until just tender. Serve the sauce over the noodles with shavings of cheese on top.

SUITABLE FOR FREEZING AFTER STEP 3

300 Calories per serving

CREAMY PASTA WITH PRAWNS AND TUNA

PREPARATION TIME: 5 minutes
COOKING TIME: 10 minutes

If there's no time to chop the basil, just stir a few leaves into the sauce as it simmers.

SERVES 4

225 g (8 oz) dried pasta shells or spirals
salt and pepper
15 ml (1 tbsp) oil
75 g (3 oz) spring onions, trimmed and sliced
1 garlic clove, skinned and crushed
30 ml (2 level tbsp) dried tomatoes, chopped,
or 5 ml (1 level tsp) tomato purée
90 ml (6 level tbsp) fromage frais or single cream
125 g (4 oz) cooked peeled prawns
200 g (7 oz) can tuna fish in brine, drained
and flaked
1 small bunch of fresh basil, chopped
spring onion shreds and basil, to garnish
(optional)

1 Cook the pasta in boiling salted water until just tender.
2 Meanwhile, heat the oil in a medium saucepan, add the onions and garlic, and stir-fry for 1 minute. Stir in the chopped tomatoes or tomato purée, fromage frais, prawns and tuna with a little chopped fresh basil and 60 ml (4 tbsp) water. Simmer for 2–3 minutes to heat through.
3 Drain the pasta, then return it to the pan. Pour over the sauce, stirring to mix. Warm gently to heat through. Adjust the seasoning and garnish with spring onion shreds and basil.

NOT SUITABLE FOR FREEZING

355 Calories per serving

TAGLIATELLE WITH TUNA AND SWEETCORN

PREPARATION TIME: 15 minutes
COOKING TIME: 15–20 minutes

Three packets of parsley sauce mix would normally make 900 ml (1½ pints) of sauce. In this recipe, only 568 ml (1 pint) of milk is used as the mushroom liquid thins the sauce down further.

SERVES 8

450 g (1 lb) dried tagliatelle
salt and pepper
three 15 g (½ oz) packets parsley sauce mix
568 ml (1 pint) milk
50 ml (2 fl oz) white wine
two 350 g (12 oz) cans sweetcorn kernels, drained
450 g (1 lb) button mushrooms, wiped and sliced
two 200 g (7 oz) cans tuna in brine
30 ml (2 level tbsp) double cream
grated Parmesan cheese and finely sliced spring
onions, to garnish

1 Cook the pasta in boiling salted water until just tender.
2 Meanwhile, in a large saucepan, prepare the sauce according to the manufacturer's instructions, but using only 568 ml (1 pint) milk. Add the wine, sweetcorn and mushrooms. Cook for a further 2 minutes, stirring occasionally.
3 Meanwhile, drain and flake the tuna, add to the sauce and heat very gently for a further 2 minutes. Stir in the cream and season.
4 To serve, drain the pasta and place in a heated serving dish. Spoon the sauce over the pasta, sprinkle with Parmesan and spring onions.

NOT SUITABLE FOR FREEZING

460 Calories per serving

Broccoli and Ham Tagliatelle

PREPARATION TIME: 5 minutes
COOKING TIME: 10 minutes

SERVES 4

225 g (8 oz) dried green or white tagliatelle
salt and pepper
50 g (2 oz) butter or margarine
125 g (4 oz) onion, skinned and sliced
225 g (8 oz) small broccoli florets
125 g (4 oz) yellow pepper, deseeded and chopped
25 g (1 oz) plain flour
568 ml (1 pint) milk
225 g (8 oz) ham, chopped
2.5 ml (½ level tsp) freshly grated nutmeg
125 g (4 oz) Cheddar cheese, grated

1 Cook the pasta in boiling salted water until just tender. Drain and cover to keep warm in the saucepan.
2 Meanwhile, melt the butter or margarine in a large saucepan, add the onion, broccoli and pepper, and fry gently until beginning to soften. Add the flour and cook for 1 minute, stirring. Remove the pan from the heat and add the milk, ham, nutmeg and seasoning. Return to the heat and bring to the boil, stirring. Cook for 1–2 minutes, then adjust the seasoning.
3 Stir the sauce through the cooked pasta and turn into a shallow, flameproof dish. Scatter over the Cheddar cheese and grill until golden.

NOT SUITABLE FOR FREEZING

695 Calories per serving

Noodles with Hot Ham and Parmesan Cheese

PREPARATION TIME: 10 minutes
COOKING TIME: 15 minutes

SERVES 4

225 g (8 oz) dried, broad pasta noodles (pappardelle)
salt and pepper
350 g (12 oz) fresh asparagus or French beans
125 g (4 oz) trimmed leeks, cut into fine shreds
142 ml (5 fl oz) carton single cream
50 g (2 oz) Parmesan cheese, freshly grated
50 g (2 oz) Parma ham or thinly sliced cooked ham, chopped

1 Cook the pasta in boiling salted water until just tender. Drain well.
2 Meanwhile, trim the asparagus or beans and divide into 7.5 cm (3 inch) lengths.
3 Cook the asparagus or beans in boiling salted water for 7–10 minutes or until just tender. Add the leeks and boil for 30 seconds, then drain well.
4 Place the cream in a small saucepan with half the cheese. Heat until just boiling, stirring.
5 Toss together the hot vegetables, pasta, ham and remaining cheese. Season and serve immediately with the parmesan cream.

NOT SUITABLE FOR FREEZING

365 Calories per serving

Pasta with Pesto

PREPARATION TIME: 15 minutes
COOKING TIME: 10 minutes

This pesto, made with fresh basil and fromage frais, has a lovely, creamy consistency. It has much more flavour and fewer calories than the bottled variety. Use fresh pasta if available.

SERVES 4

50 g (2 oz) garlic cloves, skinned
40 g (1½ oz) fresh basil
300 ml (10 fl oz) very low-fat fromage frais or quark
30 ml (2 tbsp) olive oil
salt and pepper
225 g (8 oz) dried pasta, such as tagliatelle
50 g (2 oz) Parmesan cheese
basil leaves, to garnish (optional)

1 Place the garlic cloves in a saucepan of boiling water. Reduce the heat, cover and simmer for 10 minutes or until soft. Drain well.
2 Pull the leaves off the basil stalks and put in a food processor with the garlic, fromage frais or quark, olive oil and seasoning. Blend until smooth, then adjust the seasoning.
3 Cook the pasta in boiling salted water until just tender. Drain and return to the pan. Add the sauce and stir over a moderate heat for 1–2 minutes.
4 Serve immediately, topped with shavings of fresh Parmesan cheese and garnished with fresh basil leaves, if wished.

NOT SUITABLE FOR FREEZING

370 Calories per serving

Ravioli with Gorgonzola and Rosemary Sauce

PREPARATION TIME: 5 minutes
COOKING TIME: 10 minutes

SERVES 4

450 g (1 lb) spinach and ricotta or beef ravioli, or other filled pasta shapes, such as tortellini
salt and pepper
125 g (4 oz) gorgonzola or other creamy blue cheese, such as cambozola
50 g (2 oz) medium-fat, mild cheese, such as Fontina or Edam
200 ml (7 fl oz) single cream
15 ml (1 level tbsp) chopped fresh rosemary or 5 ml (1 level tsp) dried
fresh rosemary, to garnish

1 Cook the pasta in boiling salted water until just tender. Keep in the pan with the cooking water.
2 Meanwhile, roughly chop the cheeses, discarding the rinds. Put the cream, half the cheese and the rosemary in a small saucepan. Heat together gently until the cheese has melted, stirring occasionally.
3 Add 60 ml (4 tbsp) pasta water to the cheese sauce and bring to the boil. Drain the pasta and toss with the sauce and the remaining cheese. Season with plenty of pepper and a little salt, if wished (the cheese is fairly salty). Garnish with rosemary.

NOT SUITABLE FOR FREEZING

625 Calories per serving

Ravioli with Gorgonzola and Rosemary Sauce

PASTA AND PEPPER GRATIN

PREPARATION TIME: 10 minutes
COOKING TIME: 20 minutes

SERVES 4

350 g (12 oz) large pasta shells
salt and pepper
30 ml (2 tbsp) olive oil
175 g (6 oz) low-fat soft cheese
175 g (6 oz) hummus
grated rind and strained juice of 1 lemon
142 ml (5 fl oz) carton single cream
1 green pepper, deseeded and cut into thin strips
1 red pepper, deseeded and cut into thin strips
45 ml (3 level tbsp) chopped fresh parsley
75 ml (5 level tbsp) freshly grated Parmesan cheese
flat-leaf parsley, to garnish

1 Cook the pasta shells in boiling salted water with half the oil until just tender. Drain well, shaking away excess water.
2 Meanwhile, mix together the soft cheese, hummus, lemon rind and juice, single cream and a little black pepper.
3 Heat the remaining olive oil in a large frying pan, add the peppers, and sauté for about 5 minutes, or until beginning to soften. Remove from the heat and stir in the pasta and the soft cheese mixture, with the chopped parsley.
4 Spoon into a large, shallow gratin dish and sprinkle with the Parmesan cheese. Grill under a moderate heat for about 5 minutes, or until lightly browned. Serve immediately.

NOT SUITABLE FOR FREEZING

600 Calories per serving

CAPPELLETTI WITH MUSHROOM SAUCE

PREPARATION TIME: 20 minutes
COOKING TIME: 10 minutes

You'll find dried mushrooms in Italian delicatessens and most major supermarkets. Try adding them to casseroles and soups – they have a delicious, rich flavour.

SERVES 4

25 g (1 oz) dried porcini mushrooms
300 ml (½ pint) warm water
225 g (8 oz) cappelletti or other dried pasta shapes
salt and pepper
25 g (1 oz) butter or margarine
1 onion, skinned and finely chopped
1 garlic clove, skinned and crushed
225 g (8 oz) button mushrooms, wiped and sliced
15 ml (1 level tbsp) chopped fresh chives
50 ml (2 fl oz) fromage frais

1 Soak the dried porcini in the warm water for about 20 minutes. Remove the mushrooms from the water with a slotted spoon and slice. Reserve the soaking liquid.
2 Cook the pasta in boiling, salted water until just tender.
3 Melt the butter or margarine in a frying pan, add the onion and garlic and sauté until softened. Add all the mushrooms and sauté for 3–4 minutes. Add the soaking liquid and allow to bubble over a high heat for about 4–5 minutes, or until reduced by half. Season to taste.
4 Drain the pasta well and stir into the mushroom sauce with the chives. Spoon over the fromage frais to serve.

NOT SUITABLE FOR FREEZING

290 Calories per serving

PASTA WITH BACON SAUCE

PREPARATION TIME: 10 minutes
COOKING TIME: 15 minutes

If you can, choose the wrinkly black olives for this – they have a much better flavour. And look out for frozen chopped fresh herbs in supermarkets – they can be stirred straight into the sauce while still frozen.

SERVES 4

350 g (12 oz) dried pasta, such as vermicelli, spaghetti or penne

salt and pepper

60 ml (4 tbsp) olive oil

2 garlic cloves, skinned and crushed

225 g (8 oz) smoked streaky bacon, derinded and roughly chopped

two 400 g (14 oz) cans chopped tomatoes

125 g (4 oz) black olives, preferably the wrinkly variety, pitted and roughly chopped

60 ml (4 level tbsp) chopped fresh herbs, such as basil, marjoram or parsley

chopped fresh herbs, to garnish (optional)

1 Cook the pasta in boiling salted water until just tender. Drain and toss with 30 ml (2 tbsp) olive oil. Cover and keep warm.

2 Meanwhile, heat the remaining 30 ml (2 tbsp) oil in a frying pan and fry the garlic and bacon until golden. Stir in the tomatoes, olives and herbs, and heat for 2–3 minutes or until piping hot. Adjust the seasoning.

3 Toss the bacon sauce with the hot pasta and leave, covered, for 1 minute. Toss the pasta again and serve immediately, garnished with extra chopped herbs, if wished.

NOT SUITABLE FOR FREEZING

720 Calories per serving

PASTA WITH LEEK, PANCETTA AND CREAM-CHEESE SAUCE

PREPARATION TIME: 5 minutes
COOKING TIME: 10 minutes

Pancetta is similar to bacon; it comes from the same parts of the pig, but is cured in a different way, so has a very distinct flavour. Look for it in Italian delicatessens – it's also marvellous for adding to Bolognaise sauce, threading on to kebabs, etc., and it freezes well.

SERVES 4

225 g (8 oz) cappelletti or linguini

salt and pepper

25 g (1 oz) butter or margarine

225 g (8 oz) mushrooms, wiped and thinly sliced

125 g (4 oz) leeks, trimmed and thickly sliced

125 g (4 oz) pancetta or streaky bacon, derinded and chopped

1 garlic clove, skinned and crushed

125 g (4 oz) low-fat soft cheese with garlic and herbs

30 ml (2 tbsp) milk or single cream

1 Cook the pasta in boiling salted water until just tender.

2 Meanwhile, melt the butter in a medium saucepan and stir in the mushrooms, leeks, pancetta and garlic. Sauté, stirring, for 3–4 minutes or until the leeks are just tender.

3 Reduce the heat and stir in the cheese and milk or cream until thoroughly mixed. Season to taste.

4 Drain the pasta and serve immediately with the sauce.

NOT SUITABLE FOR FREEZING

240 Calories per serving

PASTA WITH SPICY SAUSAGE AND ROASTED TOMATO SAUCE

PREPARATION TIME: 10 minutes
COOKING TIME: 20 minutes

SERVES 4

450 g (1 lb) tomatoes
450 g (1 lb) spicy pork sausages
30 ml (2 tbsp) oil
125 g (4 oz) onion, skinned and roughly chopped
10 ml (2 level tsp) dried oregano
1 garlic clove, skinned and crushed
15 ml (1 level tbsp) tomato purée
salt and pepper
Tabasco sauce, to taste
225 g (8 oz) orecchiette or cappelletti

1 Halve the tomatoes and scoop the seeds into a sieve over a small bowl. Press the seeds with a wooden spoon to extract all the juice. Reserve.
2 Place the tomato shells, skin-side up, under a hot grill and cook until well browned and blistered. Rub to remove the skins and roughly chop the flesh. Skin the sausages, if preferred, and slice thickly.
3 Heat the oil in a large saucepan and stir in the onion, oregano and garlic. Cook, stirring, for 2–3 minutes or until beginning to soften. Add the sausages and cook until browned.
4 Stir in the chopped tomatoes, reserved tomato juice, tomato purée, seasoning and Tabasco sauce. Bring to the boil, then reduce the heat, cover and simmer gently for 10–12 minutes.
5 Meanwhile, cook the orecchiette or cappelletti in boiling salted water until tender. Drain well. Adjust the seasoning of the sauce and pour over the hot pasta. Serve at once.

FREEZE AT THE END OF STEP 4

485 Calories per serving

SPAGHETTI WITH WALNUTS AND SMOKY BACON

PREPARATION TIME: 10 minutes
COOKING TIME: 10 minutes

SERVES 4

350 g (12 oz) dried spaghetti
salt and pepper
50 ml (2 fl oz) olive oil
275 g (10 oz) rindless smoked back bacon, cut into large, bite-sized pieces
1 garlic clove, skinned and crushed
75 g (3 oz) walnut pieces, roughly chopped
450 g (1 lb) tomatoes, skinned (optional) and chopped
60 ml (4 level tbsp) chopped flat-leaf parsley
grated rind of 1 lemon
225 g (8 oz) soft cheese, such as goat's cheese in olive oil

1 Cook the pasta in boiling, salted water until just tender.
2 Meanwhile, heat the oil in a large sauté pan and sauté the bacon, garlic and walnuts together until golden brown, stirring occasionally. Stir in the tomatoes, parsley and grated lemon rind. Heat, stirring, for 1–2 minutes or until piping hot. Season with black pepper.
3 Drain the pasta and toss with the walnut and bacon sauce. Serve immediately, topping each portion with pieces of soft cheese.

NOT SUITABLE FOR FREEZING

730 Calories per serving

Spaghetti with Walnuts and Smoky Bacon

SUMMER PASTA

PREPARATION TIME: 10 minutes
COOKING TIME: 10 minutes

SERVES 4

450 g (1 lb) tomatoes, deseeded and roughly
chopped
grated rind of 1 lemon
45 ml (3 tbsp) balsamic vinegar
salt and pepper
225 g (8 oz) dried pasta noodles, e.g. pappardelle
15 ml (1 tbsp) olive oil
15 ml (1 level tbsp) chopped fresh thyme
225 g (8 oz) mozzarella cheese, diced

1 Put the tomatoes in a saucepan with the lemon rind, balsamic vinegar and seasoning.
2 Cook the pasta in boiling salted water until just tender. Drain well. Toss in the olive oil with the thyme.
3 Warm the tomato mixture for 2–3 minutes and spoon over the pasta. Top with mozzarella cheese and serve immediately.

NOT SUITABLE FOR FREEZING

410 Calories per serving

CHICKEN AND BACON PASTA

PREPARATION TIME: 10 minutes
COOKING TIME: 15 minutes

SERVES 4

225 g (8 oz) chicken livers, trimmed
350 g (12 oz) skinless chicken breast fillets
200 g (7 oz) back bacon, derinded
30 ml (2 tbsp) oil
2 garlic cloves, skinned and crushed
225 g (8 oz) dried pasta shells
400 g (14 oz) can of chopped tomatoes
150 ml (¼ pint) chicken stock
15 ml (1 tbsp) sherry
2.5 ml (½ level tsp) dried rosemary
salt and pepper
12 pitted mixed olives (optional)
parsley and rosemary sprigs, to garnish

1 Roughly chop the chicken livers, chicken fillets and bacon into bite-sized pieces.
2 Heat the oil in a large sauté pan, add the chicken, bacon and garlic, and cook for about 5 minutes or until golden brown.
3 Cook the pasta shells in boiling salted water until just tender.
4 Meanwhile, add the tomatoes, stock, sherry and rosemary to the sauté pan. Season with salt and pepper, bring to the boil and simmer for 2–3 minutes.
5 Stir in the chicken livers and olives, if using. Cook gently for a further 4–5 minutes or until the chicken livers are tender and the sauce has thickened slightly.
6 Drain the pasta and transfer to a warmed serving dish. Spoon the sauce on top, garnish with parsley and rosemary, and serve immediately.

NOT SUITABLE FOR FREEZING

612 Calories per serving

CLASSIC TOMATO PASTA

PREPARATION TIME: 5 minutes

COOKING TIME: 25–30 minutes

The basic pasta sauce in this recipe can be made in batches and frozen.

SERVES 4

15 ml (1 tbsp) olive oil

75 g (3 oz) onion, skinned and chopped

75 g (3 oz) carrots, peeled and sliced

75 g (3 oz) celery, trimmed and sliced

1 garlic clove, skinned and crushed

two 400 g (14 oz) cans chopped tomatoes

30 ml (2 level tbsp) tomato purée

150 ml (¼ pint) chicken or vegetable stock

100 ml (4 fl oz) red wine

salt and pepper

350 g (12 oz) dried pasta

50 g (2 oz) sun-dried tomatoes, in olive oil (drained weight), finely chopped

freshly grated Parmesan cheese, to serve

1 Heat the olive oil in a large saucepan, add the vegetables and garlic, and cook, stirring continuously, for 5 minutes or until beginning to soften but not colour.

2 Stir in the canned tomatoes, tomato purée, stock, wine and seasoning, cover and simmer for about 20 minutes, stirring occasionally.

3 Meanwhile, cook the pasta in boiling salted water until just tender. Purée the sauce in a food processor, then return to a clean saucepan and stir in the sun-dried tomatoes.

4 Adjust the seasoning and reheat the sauce before serving with the hot drained pasta. Top with Parmesan cheese.

SAUCE CAN BE FROZEN AT THE END OF STEP 3

450 Calories per serving

LIGHT LEEK AND PRAWN SHELLS

PREPARATION TIME: 10 minutes

COOKING TIME: 15 minutes

You could use a flavoured cottage cheese – with chives, for example – for the filling.

SERVES 4

125 g (4 oz) large pasta shells (about 20)

salt and pepper

1 quantity Parmesan sauce (see Ricotta and Spinach Gnocchi, page 77)

10 ml (2 tsp) oil

350 g (12 oz) trimmed leeks, thinly sliced

125 g (4 oz) cooked peeled prawns

10 ml (2 tsp) lemon juice

125 g (4 oz) cottage cheese

1 Cook the pasta in boiling, salted water until just tender. Drain well and place in a shallow, flameproof dish.

2 Make the Parmesan sauce (see page 77) and keep warm. Heat the oil in a large frying pan, add the leeks and cook for 2–3 minutes or until soft and golden brown. Stir in the prawns and lemon juice, and sauté for a further 1–2 minutes or until all excess moisture is driven off. Off the heat, stir in the cottage cheese and season to taste.

3 Fill each pasta shell with the leek mixture and place in a flameproof dish. Spoon over the sauce and place under a hot grill until golden brown.

NOT SUITABLE FOR FREEZING

300 Calories per serving

*T*HREE-CHEESE MACARONI

PREPARATION TIME: 10 minutes
COOKING TIME: 20 minutes

This is the ultimate macaroni cheese. It uses three cheeses: Italian Fontina, a mild, buttery cheese, for flavour; mozzarella, for its creaminess and texture; and freshly grated Parmesan, which adds its distinctive 'bite'. You can substitute either Gouda or Edam, if you can't find Fontina.

SERVES 4

225 g (8 oz) macaroni
salt and pepper
50 g (2 oz) butter
40 g (1½ oz) plain flour
1 bay leaf
900 ml (1½ pints) milk (preferably semi-skimmed)
225 g (8 oz) Fontina, Gouda or Edam cheese, coarsely grated
10 ml (2 level tsp) Dijon mustard
a large pinch of freshly grated nutmeg
125 g (4 oz) mozzarella cheese, roughly chopped
50 g (2 oz) Parmesan cheese, freshly grated

15 g (½ oz) fresh white breadcrumbs
flat-leaf parsley, to garnish

1 Cook the macaroni in boiling salted water until just tender. Drain and set aside.
2 Melt the butter in a medium saucepan and stir in the flour and bay leaf. Cook, stirring, for 1–2 minutes, before adding the milk. Bring to the boil, stirring all the time until lightly thickened. Remove the bay leaf.
3 Off the heat, beat in the Fontina cheese and mustard. Season the sauce with a little salt and pepper and the grated nutmeg. Fold in the cooked macaroni, mozzarella and 25 g (1 oz) Parmesan. Stir over a gentle heat until piping hot.
4 Spoon into a lightly greased, shallow 2.3 litre (3 pint) flameproof dish. Sprinkle with the remaining grated Parmesan and the breadcrumbs.
5 Flash under a hot grill to brown. Serve immediately, garnished with flat-leaf parsley.

NOT SUITABLE FOR FREEZING

770 Calories per serving

SNAPPY SALADS

WARM PASTA SALAD

PREPARATION TIME: 5 minutes
COOKING TIME: 8 minutes

Tossing the ingredients together while the pasta is still warm helps the flavours to mix well.

SERVES 4

350 g (12 oz) dried pasta spirals
salt and pepper
1 red pepper
1 green pepper
200 g (7 oz) can tuna in brine, drained
45 ml (3 level tbsp) natural yogurt
green salad with a squeeze of lemon juice,
to serve

1 Cook the pasta in boiling salted water until just tender, then drain. Meanwhile, deseed and chop both the peppers, and flake the tuna.
2 Place the warm pasta in a serving dish and stir in the peppers, tuna and yogurt. Season to taste with plenty of pepper.
3 Serve immediately accompanied by a green salad sharpened with a squeeze of lemon juice.

NOT SUITABLE FOR FREEZING

370 Calories per serving

CHICKEN AND HAM PASTA SALAD

PREPARATION TIME: 10 minutes
COOKING TIME: 10 minutes

SERVES 8

225 g (8 oz) dried pasta bows
salt and pepper
225 g (8 oz) mangetouts, trimmed
125 g (4 oz) smoked cooked ham
450 g (1 lb) cooked chicken breast fillets
150 g (5 oz) natural yogurt
45 ml (3 tbsp) French dressing
400 g (14 oz) can pitted black olives,
drained and halved

1 Cook the pasta in boiling salted water until just tender, adding the mangetouts for the last 2 minutes of cooking. Drain well and cool under cold running water.
2 Slice the ham and chicken, discarding any fat or skin. Mix with the pasta and mangetouts.
3 Mix together the yogurt and French dressing. Add the olives to the salad, pour over the dressing, and toss well to coat. Season and serve at once.

NOT SUITABLE FOR FREEZING

290 Calories per serving

*W*INTER SALAD

PREPARATION TIME: 10 minutes
COOKING TIME: nil

SERVES 4

1 lemon
30 ml (2 tbsp) olive oil
150 ml (5 fl oz) natural yogurt
salt and pepper
2 apples, cored and roughly chopped
225 g (8 oz) red cabbage, finely sliced
1 small onion, skinned and finely sliced
4 celery sticks, trimmed and finely sliced
125 g (4 oz) Cheddar cheese, cubed
50 g (2 oz) unsalted peanuts in skins
celery leaves, to garnish (optional)

1 Grate the rind of half the lemon into a large bowl. Squeeze the juice from the lemon and add 45 ml (3 tbsp) to the lemon rind. Add the olive oil and yogurt, and whisk everything together. Season well.
2 Toss the apples in the dressing, then add the cabbage, onion, celery and cheese. Toss all the ingredients with the apples, mixing well. Sprinkle with peanuts and garnish with celery leaves, if using.

NOT SUITABLE FOR FREEZING

335 Calories per serving

*H*OT SPICED CHICK PEA SALAD

PREPARATION TIME: 5 minutes
COOKING TIME: 10 minutes

SERVES 4

15 ml (1 tbsp) oil
125 g (4 oz) onion, skinned and roughly chopped
10 ml (2 level tsp) ground turmeric
15 ml (1 level tbsp) cumin seeds
450 g (1 lb) tomatoes, roughly chopped
two 400 g (14 oz) cans chick peas, drained and rinsed
15 ml (1 tbsp) lemon juice
60 ml (4 level tbsp) chopped fresh coriander
salt and pepper
coriander leaves, to garnish

1 Heat the oil in a saucepan and sauté the onion until golden brown.
2 Add the turmeric and cumin seeds, and cook, stirring, for 1–2 minutes before adding the remaining ingredients.
3 Sauté for 1–2 minutes, stirring frequently, then adjust the seasoning. Serve garnished with fresh coriander.

NOT SUITABLE FOR FREEZING

345 Calories per serving

Hot Spiced Chick Pea Salad

*W*ILD MUSHROOM AND LENTIL SALAD

PREPARATION TIME: 15 minutes
COOKING TIME: 5 minutes

SERVES 4

350 g (12 oz) brown-cap or wild mushrooms
selection of salad leaves, e.g. rocket, endive
5 ml (1 tsp) walnut oil
50 g (2 oz) lean smoked back bacon, derinded
and cut into strips
salt and pepper
5 ml (1 level tsp) chopped fresh tarragon
150 ml (5 fl oz) low-fat bio natural yogurt
5 ml (1 tsp) runny honey
cayenne pepper
50 g (2 oz) alfalfa sprouts
125 g (4 oz) sprouting lentils

1 Rinse the mushrooms in cold water, then pat dry. Halve if necessary. Rinse and dry the salad.
2 Gently heat the walnut oil in a frying pan, add the bacon strips and fry until crisp. Remove with a slotted spoon and drain on absorbent kitchen paper. Add the mushrooms to the pan and sauté until slightly softened. Season with salt and pepper. Remove with a slotted spoon and drain on absorbent kitchen paper, reserving the pan juices to add to the dressing.
3 Combine the chopped tarragon, yogurt, honey and pan juices. Season with salt and a pinch of cayenne pepper to taste.
4 Arrange the salad, alfalfa sprouts, lentils, bacon and mushrooms on six plates. Spoon a little dressing on the side.

NOT SUITABLE FOR FREEZING

80 Calories per serving

*G*RILLED CHICORY AND ASPARAGUS SALAD

PREPARATION TIME: 3 minutes
COOKING TIME: 5 minutes

SERVES 1

1 small head of chicory
75 g (3 oz) thin asparagus, trimmed
salt and pepper
25 g (1 oz) Parmesan cheese, freshly grated
sprigs of fresh thyme, to garnish (optional)
15 ml (1 level tbsp) mayonnaise and
1 small toasted brown roll, buttered, to serve

1 Break up the chicory and place in a flame-proof serving dish.
2 Cook the asparagus in boiling salted water for 2–3 minutes or until just tender. Drain and place on top of the chicory. Sprinkle over the grated Parmesan.
3 Place the asparagus and chicory under a medium grill for 2–3 minutes or until the cheese starts to melt. Garnish with sprigs of fresh thyme, if using.
4 Serve with mayonnaise and a toasted brown roll.

NOT SUITABLE FOR FREEZING

432 Calories per serving (with mayonnaise and roll)

Warm Vegetable Salad

PREPARATION TIME: 10 minutes
COOKING TIME: 3 minutes

You can use whatever vegetables you have available for this recipe. If you can't find bobby beans, use French beans instead.

SERVES 2

50 g (2 oz) carrots, peeled
2 courgettes, trimmed
50 g (2 oz) bobby beans, topped and tailed
50 g (2 oz) mangetouts, topped and tailed
50 g (2 oz) broccoli florets
salt and pepper
7.5 ml (1½ level tsp) Dijon mustard
15 ml (1 tbsp) lemon juice
45 ml (3 level tbsp) mayonnaise
125 g (4 oz) cold cooked chicken meat, skinned
chive flowers, to garnish (optional)

1 Cut the carrots into thin batons, slice the courgettes, and cut the beans into 2.5 cm (1 inch) lengths. Cook all the vegetables in boiling salted water for 3 minutes, then drain.
2 Stir the Dijon mustard and lemon juice into the mayonnaise and season well. Mix with the vegetables and spoon on to individual serving plates. Place strips of cold chicken on top of the vegetables and serve immediately, garnished with chive flowers if wished.

NOT SUITABLE FOR FREEZING

295 Calories per serving

Spinach, Bacon and Omelette Salad

PREPARATION TIME: 5 minutes
COOKING TIME: 8 minutes

Try to find small young spinach leaves as they are more tender than older leaves.

SERVES 2

125 g (4 oz) ready-prepared spinach
4 rashers of lean back bacon, derinded
5 ml (1 tsp) oil
2 eggs, beaten
salt and pepper
4 anchovy fillets
60 ml (4 tbsp) fat-free vinaigrette dressing
fresh chervil, to garnish (optional)

1 Tear the spinach into small pieces and place in a bowl.
2 Grill the bacon until quite crisp, then drain on absorbent kitchen paper. Snip into small pieces and sprinkle over the spinach.
3 Heat the oil in a small non-stick frying pan and add the eggs. Season with plenty of pepper and fry until quite firm. Drain on absorbent kitchen paper, then slice into strips and mix into the spinach.
4 Mash or shred the anchovy fillets and mix with the dressing. Toss into the salad. Serve immediately, garnished with fresh chervil, if using.

NOT SUITABLE FOR FREEZING

495 Calories per serving

Overleaf: Left to right: Grilled Chicory and Asparagus Salad; Warm Vegetable Salad; Spinach, Bacon and Omelette Salad

*P*ASTA SALAD WITH CHICKEN AND PESTO

PREPARATION TIME: 15 minutes
COOKING TIME: 10 minutes

SERVES 4

175 g (6 oz) mixed tomato, spinach and egg
pasta spirals
salt and pepper
15 ml (1 tbsp) olive oil
15 ml (1 level tbsp) pesto sauce
1 garlic clove, skinned and crushed
6 spring onions, trimmed and sliced
1 bulb of Florence fennel, sliced
125 g (4 oz) cooked chicken meat, cut into strips
75 g (3 oz) cooked cured ham, cut into strips
175 g (6 oz) cherry tomatoes, halved
8 pitted black olives, halved
30 ml (2 level tbsp) chopped fresh mixed herbs
15 ml (1 level tbsp) toasted pine nuts

1 Cook the pasta spirals in boiling salted water until just tender.
2 Meanwhile, gently heat the oil, pesto sauce and garlic together in a small saucepan.
3 Drain the pasta and turn into a bowl. Pour over the pesto mixture and toss well. Leave to cool.
4 Add the spring onions, fennel, chicken, ham, tomatoes and olives to the cooled pasta, and season well.
5 Turn into a serving bowl and sprinkle over the herbs and toasted pine nuts.

NOT SUITABLE FOR FREEZING

300 Calories per serving

*B*EEF SALAD WITH HORSERADISH DRESSING

PREPARATION TIME: 5 minutes
COOKING TIME: nil

A simple yet tasty salad which will satisfy the healthiest appetite.

SERVES 2

10 ml (2 level tsp) creamed horseradish sauce
30 ml (2 tbsp) vinaigrette dressing
salt and pepper
mixed salad leaves
3 medium tomatoes, sliced
175 g (6 oz) cold roast beef
mint leaves, to garnish

1 Stir the horseradish sauce into the vinaigrette dressing. Season well and mix thoroughly.
2 Arrange the salad leaves and tomatoes on two serving plates.
3 Trim the beef, cut into wafer-thin slices and place on top of the salad. Spoon over the dressing and garnish with mint leaves.

NOT SUITABLE FOR FREEZING

285 Calories per serving

WARM LAMB SALAD

PREPARATION TIME: 10 minutes
COOKING TIME: 10 minutes

SERVES 4

four 125 g (4 oz) leg of lamb steaks
150 ml (¼ pint) vegetable oil
60 ml (4 tbsp) fresh orange juice
15 ml (1 level tbsp) wholegrain mustard
salt and pepper
350 g (12 oz) trimmed leeks, thinly sliced
350 g (12 oz) spring cabbage greens, trimmed
and thinly sliced
75 g (3 oz) beansprouts
50 g (2 oz) toasted walnut pieces
crusty bread, to serve

1 Brush the lamb steaks with a little of the oil and grill for about 4 minutes on each side. Cut into thick slices.
2 To make the dressing, whisk the remaining oil with the orange juice, mustard and seasoning. Heat in a large saucepan, then add the leeks and cabbage, and cook over a high heat for 3–4 minutes or until just tender, stirring frequently. Add the beansprouts, walnuts and lamb and continue to cook for 1 minute. Serve with slices of crusty bread.

NOT SUITABLE FOR FREEZING

660 Calories per serving

SALADE NIÇOISE

PREPARATION TIME: 10–15 minutes
COOKING TIME: 20 minutes

This salad is delicious hot or cold (cool the vegetables before tossing).

SERVES 4

450 g (1 lb) small new potatoes
salt and pepper
125 g (4 oz) French beans, topped and tailed
2 eggs, hard-boiled
4 ripe tomatoes, roughly chopped
50 g (2 oz) pitted black olives
200 g (7 oz) can tuna in brine, drained
15 g (½ oz) canned anchovies, drained
30 ml (2 tbsp) oil
15 ml (1 tbsp) white wine vinegar
pinch of sugar
pinch of mustard powder
5 ml (1 tsp) lemon juice
mixed salad leaves

1 Cook the potatoes in boiling salted water for 15–20 minutes, or until tender. Cook the French beans in boiling salted water for 3 minutes, or until just tender.
2 Shell the eggs and cut into wedges. Toss together the potatoes, beans, tomatoes, eggs, olives and tuna and top with anchovies.
3 Whisk together the remaining ingredients, except the salad leaves, and season to taste. Pile the vegetable mixture on a bed of mixed salad leaves and pour over the dressing.

NOT SUITABLE FOR FREEZING

225 Calories per serving

Garlic Croûton Salad

PREPARATION TIME: 3 minutes
COOKING TIME: 5 minutes

French bread looks attractive here, but could be replaced with quarters of toasted white bread.

Serves 1

25 g (1 oz) French bread
1 garlic clove, skinned and halved
40 g (1½ oz) low-fat garlic and herb soft cheese
mixed salad leaves
salt and pepper

1 Cut the bread into three or four thin slices. Toast on both sides.
2 Rub one side of each slice with the cut garlic, then spread the soft cheese on the same side. Grill gently until the cheese browns slightly.
3 Arrange the salad leaves on a plate and place the croûtons on top. Season and serve immediately.

NOT SUITABLE FOR FREEZING

200 Calories per serving

Grilled Tomato and Mozzarella Salad

PREPARATION TIME: 10 minutes
COOKING TIME: 10 minutes

All too often, tomatoes are under-ripe and have little taste. If you're buying from a supermarket, look for the packs marked 'grown for flavour' – it does make a difference. This salad can be prepared ahead, chilled, then grilled just before serving. Watch the aubergine slices don't overbrown.

Serves 4

175 g (6 oz) aubergine, thinly sliced
45 ml (3 tbsp) olive oil
60 ml (4 level tbsp) roughly chopped fresh basil
finely grated rind and juice of 1 lemon
salt and pepper
450 g (1 lb) tomatoes, skinned (optional) and thinly sliced
150 g (5 oz) mozzarella cheese, thinly sliced
fresh basil leaves, to garnish

1 Brush the aubergine slices very lightly with some of the olive oil and grill on both sides until they are crisp and golden brown. Don't let them get too dark at this stage.
2 Whisk together the remaining olive oil, the roughly chopped basil, lemon rind and 5 ml (1 tsp) lemon juice. Season with plenty of salt and pepper.
3 Arrange the aubergine, tomato and mozzarella slices, overlapping in a single layer, in a large, shallow, flameproof dish. Spoon the dressing over. Place under a hot grill for 3–4 minutes or until the mozzarella begins to melt. Serve immediately, seasoned with extra salt and pepper and garnished with fresh basil leaves.

NOT SUITABLE FOR FREEZING

240 Calories per serving

Grilled Tomato and Mozzarella Salad

Bean and Tuna Salad

PREPARATION TIME: 10 minutes
COOKING TIME: 10 minutes

This substantial salad is ideal for a quick healthy snack.

SERVES 3–4

175 g (6 oz) frozen French beans
salt and pepper
125 g (4 oz) onion, skinned and thinly sliced
400 g (14 oz) can flageolet beans or chick peas, drained and rinsed
30 ml (2 tbsp) oil (preferably olive)
10 ml (2 tsp) vinegar (preferably white wine)
200 g (7 oz) can tuna, drained and roughly flaked
chopped fresh parsley (optional)
bread (preferably Granary), to serve

1 Cook the beans in boiling salted water until just tender. Drain and cool under cold running water. Halve if large.

2 Place the onion in a saucepan of cold water and bring to the boil, then reduce the heat and simmer for 2 minutes. Drain and then cool quickly under cold running water.

3 Place the French beans and onion in a bowl with the flageolet beans or chick peas. Add the oil and vinegar, and season with salt and pepper.

4 Add the tuna to the bowl and toss lightly to mix. Sprinkle with parsley, if using, and serve with thick chunks of Granary bread.

NOT SUITABLE FOR FREEZING

465 Calories per serving for 3
350 Calories per serving for 4

Smoked Mackerel Salad with Yogurt and Orange

PREPARATION TIME: 5 minutes
COOKING TIME: nil

The tangy yogurt and orange dressing cuts through the richness of the smoked mackerel.

SERVES 2

watercress and lamb's tongue lettuce
175 g (6 oz) smoked mackerel fillets, skinned
grated rind and juice of 1 small orange
90 ml (6 level tbsp) natural yogurt
10 ml (2 level tsp) creamed horseradish sauce
salt and pepper
2 slices of brown toast, to serve

1 Place the watercress and lettuce on two individual serving plates. Place the mackerel fillets on top of each serving of salad.

2 Whisk the orange rind, 30 ml (2 tbsp) orange juice, the yogurt and horseradish together. Season to taste.

3 Spoon the dressing over the mackerel and serve with toast.

NOT SUITABLE FOR FREEZING

240 Calories per serving

Smoked salmon salad

PREPARATION TIME: 5 minutes

COOKING TIME: nil

SERVES 2

mixed salad leaves
2 bagels
50 g (2 oz) low-fat soft cheese
¼ cucumber, sliced
50 g (2 oz) smoked salmon, sliced
½ lemon
black pepper

1 Divide the salad leaves between two individual serving plates. Halve the bagels and spread each half thinly with soft cheese. Top with slices of cucumber followed by slices of smoked salmon.

2 Place two bagel halves on each plate. Squeeze over a little lemon juice and grind over plenty of black pepper.

NOT SUITABLE FOR FREEZING

245 Calories per serving

SWEET SURPRISES

CARAMELISED APPLE WAFER

PREPARATION TIME: 10–15 minutes
COOKING TIME: 20 minutes

The tops of the apple slices and the pastry edges will look very dark.

SERVES 6

125 g (4 oz) puff pastry, thawed if frozen
6 small Granny Smith apples, about 450–700 g
(1–1½ lb) total weight
75 g (3 oz) butter or margarine, melted
60 ml (4 level tbsp) demerara sugar
Greek-style natural yogurt, to serve

1 Halve the pastry, then, on a lightly floured surface, roll it out very thinly to give two rectangles about 20.5 × 11.5 cm (8 × 4½ inches). Trim the edges.
2 Peel and halve the apples, and remove the cores. Thinly slice the apple halves but not quite through to the base. The apples should retain their shape. Evenly space six halves, flat-side down, on each pastry base to cover completely. Slice both rectangles into three and place on a baking sheet.
3 Brush the apple with the butter or margarine and sprinkle over the demerara sugar.
4 Bake in the oven at 240°C (475°F) mark 9 for about 20 minutes or until the apples are soft and caramelised. Serve immediately with Greek-style natural yogurt.

NOT SUITABLE FOR FREEZING

280 Calories per serving

RASPBERRY RICE

PREPARATION TIME: 3 minutes
COOKING TIME: 5 minutes

SERVES 6

370 g (13 oz) can raspberries in natural juice,
drained
30 ml (2 level tbsp) fruits of the forest jam
two 425 g (15 oz) cans rice pudding
freshly grated nutmeg

1 Put the raspberries and jam in a food processor and purée until smooth. Sieve.
2 Put the rice pudding in a saucepan, heat gently, then allow to simmer for 2–3 minutes, stirring occasionally. Spoon into individual serving dishes.

3 Pour the fruit sauce over the rice, and serve immediately, sprinkled with nutmeg.

NOT SUITABLE FOR FREEZING

160 Calories per serving

VARIATION

For a change, stir a chopped eating apple into the rice pudding.

LEMON BRÛLÉE

PREPARATION TIME: 2 minutes
COOKING TIME: 2 minutes

You can serve the brûlée on its own or use it to top slices of fresh orange.

SERVES 4

finely grated rind of 1 lemon
450 g (1 lb) Greek-style yogurt
30 ml (2 level tbsp) dark soft brown sugar

1 Mix together the lemon rind and yogurt.
2 Divide between four 150 ml (¼ pint) ramekin dishes and sprinkle over the sugar.
3 Place under a hot grill for 1–2 minutes or until the sugar has melted and is bubbling.
4 Chill until ready to serve.

NOT SUITABLE FOR FREEZING

160 Calories per serving

PEACH CLAFOUTIS

PREPARATION TIME: 5 minutes
COOKING TIME: 25–30 minutes

SERVES 4

410 g (14½ oz) can peach halves in juice, drained
15 ml (1 level tbsp) self-raising flour
2 eggs, beaten
425 g (15 oz) can or carton custard
25 g (1 oz) toasted flaked almonds

1 Place the peaches on absorbent kitchen paper and pat dry.
2 Beat the flour and eggs together until smooth, then whisk into the custard, mixing well.
3 Arrange the peaches in a 22 cm (8 inch) flan dish. Pour over the custard mixture and spread evenly.
4 Bake in the oven at 200°C (400°F) mark 6 for 25–30 minutes. Decorate with the almonds.

NOT SUITABLE FOR FREEZING

265 Calories per serving

VARIATION

For extra speed, this clafoutis can be cooked in the microwave. Use a flan dish suitable for use in the microwave, fill with the peaches and custard as above, and cook on a turntable on HIGH for 8 minutes. Leave to stand for 5 minutes to allow the centre to finish cooking.

Warm Banana and Apricot Fruit Salad

PREPARATION TIME: 5 minutes
COOKING TIME: 8 minutes

Don't overcook the bananas – they should still retain their shape.

SERVES 4

grated rind and juice of 1 orange
15 ml (1 level tbsp) dark soft brown sugar
30 ml (2 tbsp) rum
3 large bananas, about 700 g (1½ lb) total weight
50 g (2 oz) no-soak dried apricots
natural yogurt, to serve

1 Gently heat the orange rind with 60 ml (4 tbsp) orange juice, the sugar and rum in a large frying pan.
2 Peel the bananas and cut into 0.5 cm (¼ inch) diagonal slices. Cut the apricots into shreds. Add both to the pan and bubble up, stirring gently, until coated and warmed through.
3 Serve with natural yogurt.

NOT SUITABLE FOR FREEZING

150 Calories per serving

Pears with Butterscotch Sauce

PREPARATION TIME: 5 minutes
COOKING TIME: 5 minutes

If you don't have stem ginger, use 1.25 ml (¼ level tsp) ground ginger with an additional 30 ml (2 tbsp) water.

SERVES 4

4 ripe pears, peeled, halved and cored, or two 400 g (14 oz) cans pear halves in natural juice, drained
125 g (4 oz) soft light brown sugar
30 ml (2 tbsp) syrup taken from a jar of stem ginger
300 ml (10 fl oz) Greek-style yogurt
pistachio nuts, to decorate (optional)
vanilla, chocolate-chip or toffee ice cream, to serve

1 Divide the pear halves between four serving dishes.
2 Place the sugar in a small saucepan with the syrup and 30 ml (2 tbsp) water. Heat gently until the sugar has dissolved, then boil for 1 minute. Remove from the heat and stir in the yogurt.
3 Spoon the sauce over the pears immediately, or chill until thick and fudge-like. Sprinkle with nuts, if using. Serve with ice cream.

NOT SUITABLE FOR FREEZING

285 Calories per serving

Creamy Fudge Whip

PREPARATION TIME: 5 minutes
COOKING TIME: nil

SERVES 4

150 ml (5 fl oz) double cream
150 g (5 oz) fudge yogurt or similar
1 egg white
1 chocolate-covered, finger-sized fudge bar, to decorate

1 Whip the cream until it just holds its shape. Fold in the yogurt.

2 Whisk the egg white until stiff but not dry and fold into the cream mixture. Divide between four long-stemmed wine glasses.

3 Peel strips from the fudge bar using a potato peeler and use to decorate the fudge whips.

NOT SUITABLE FOR FREEZING

250 Calories per serving

APRICOT AND ORANGE CUSTARDS

PREPARATION TIME: 15 minutes

COOKING TIME: nil

We liked the tangy flavour of these light custards, but add a little sugar if you find apricots too sharp.

SERVES 6

454 g (16 oz) carton natural fromage frais
500 g (17.6 oz) carton fresh custard sauce
finely grated rind and strained juice of 2 oranges
400 g (14 oz) can apricots in natural juice
caster sugar, to taste (optional)
sweet biscuits and single cream, to serve

1 Whisk together the fromage frais and the custard sauce until blended.

2 Stir the orange rind into the custard mixture with 60 ml (4 tbsp) strained orange juice. Mix thoroughly.

3 Drain the apricots, place in a food processor and blend until quite smooth. Add caster sugar to taste, if wished.

4 Spoon the custard into six tall, stemmed glasses and top each with apricot purée. Serve with sweet biscuits and single cream.

NOT SUITABLE FOR FREEZING

265 Calories per serving

POACHED PEARS

PREPARATION TIME: 10 minutes

COOKING TIME: 10 minutes

SERVES 4

juice of ½ lemon
4 firm pears
300 ml (½ pint) unsweetened apple juice
1 sachet of mulling spices (see Note)
pared rind and juice of 1 orange
mint leaves, to decorate
30 ml (2 level tbsp) fromage frais, to serve

1 Strain the lemon juice into a large saucepan. Peel, core and quarter the pears, add to the lemon juice and turn to coat.

2 Add the apple juice, mulling spices, orange rind and orange juice, reserving a little pared orange rind, and bring to simmering point. Partially cover and simmer for 7–10 minutes, depending on the ripeness of the pears. They should remain firm yet be tender.

3 Remove the lid. Leave the pears to cool in the liquid, then remove the mulling sachet. Decorate with mint leaves and pared orange rind, and serve with fromage frais.

NOT SUITABLE FOR FREEZING

100 Calories per serving

Note

For a sachet of mulling spices, break 1 cinnamon stick into four pieces, and place in a muslin bag with 3 cloves and 2.5 ml (½ level tsp) ground mixed spice.

CHERRY AND STRAWBERRY SAUTÉ

PREPARATION TIME: 10 minutes
COOKING TIME: 2 minutes

This recipe works very well with slightly overripe strawberries.

SERVES 4

450 g (1 lb) strawberries, hulled
450 g (1 lb) cherries, stoned
2 limes
25 g (1 oz) butter
caster sugar
15 ml (1 tbsp) balsamic vinegar
Greek-style yogurt, to serve

1 Halve or quarter the strawberries and mix with the cherries. Grate the rind and squeeze the juice from one of the limes. Mix into the fruit. Slice the remaining lime.
2 Melt the butter in a large saucepan, then add the fruit mixture, 30 ml (2 level tbsp) sugar and the lime slices. Stir in the vinegar and fry over a high heat, stirring gently, for 1–2 minutes only. Adjust the sweetness to taste and serve warm with Greek yogurt.

NOT SUITABLE FOR FREEZING

160 Calories per serving

Cherry and Strawberry Sauté

*P*EACH AND BANANA MILLEFEUILLE

PREPARATION TIME: 8 minutes
COOKING TIME: 16–18 minutes

Don't worry if the bananas discolour slightly – even when sliced at the last minute, they tend to turn brown.

SERVES 8

175 g (6 oz) puff pastry, thawed if frozen
450 g (1 lb) ripe peaches or nectarines
350 g (12 oz) firm bananas
40 g (1½ oz) butter, melted
45 ml (3 level tbsp) demerara sugar
60 ml (4 level tbsp) apricot jam

1 Roll out the pastry on a lightly floured surface to a 28 cm (11 inch) round. Place on a non-stick baking sheet and prick well. Bake in the oven at 230°C (450°F) mark 8 for 8–10 minutes or until well browned and cooked through.
2 Meanwhile, quarter, stone and roughly slice the peaches or nectarines. Peel and roughly slice the bananas.
3 Brush some of the melted butter over the pastry and scatter over the fruit. Sprinkle with sugar and drizzle with the remaining butter. Grill for 8 minutes or until the fruit is tinged with colour. Cool slightly.
4 Warm the apricot jam in a saucepan, and brush over the fruit to glaze. Leave to cool completely.

NOT SUITABLE FOR FREEZING

205 Calories per serving

*W*ALNUT AND ORANGE PUDDINGS

PREPARATION TIME: 8 minutes
COOKING TIME: 20 minutes

Walnut pieces are cheaper than whole walnuts; unless quite small, they'll need to be chopped a little further for this recipe.

SERVES 6

125 g (4 oz) soft-tub margarine
50 g (2 oz) walnut pieces, finely chopped
75 g (3 oz) caster sugar
15 ml (1 level tbsp) golden syrup
2 eggs
5 ml (1 tsp) vanilla essence
75 g (3 oz) self-raising flour
5 ml (1 level tsp) baking powder
grated rind and juice of 1 orange
custard, to serve

1 Grease six 150 ml (¼ pint) ovenproof ramekin dishes.
2 Place all the ingredients together in a large bowl with 60 ml (4 tbsp) orange juice. Beat until smooth.
3 Fill the ramekins two-thirds full with the mixture. Place on a baking sheet and bake in the oven at 180°C (350°F) mark 4 for 20–25 minutes or until firm to the touch.
4 Turn out, if wished, to serve warm with custard.

NOT SUITABLE FOR FREEZING

340 Calories per serving

*P*RUNE AND NUT CRUMBLE

PREPARATION TIME: 10 minutes
COOKING TIME: 20–25 minutes

If you can't find blackcurrant tea bags, add pared lemon rind to the reducing syrup.

SERVES 4

two 440 g (15½ oz) cans prunes in syrup, or
1 can prunes and 1 can apple slices
2 blackcurrant tea bags
225 g (8 oz) crumble mix
40 g (1½ oz) walnut pieces
soft brown sugar

1 Drain the syrup from one can of prunes into a small saucepan. Add the tea bags and boil the syrup to reduce by about half. Remove the tea bags.
2 Drain the second can of prunes or apple slices, discarding the syrup. If wished, stone all the fruit. Place the prunes and apple, if using, in a 1.1 litre (2 pint) soufflé-type dish with the reduced syrup.
3 Scatter half the crumble over the fruit, sprinkle on the walnuts, then finish with the rest of the crumble. Dredge with soft brown sugar.
4 Bake in the oven at 190°C (375°F) mark 5 for 20–25 minutes or until golden.

NOT SUITABLE FOR FREEZING

515 Calories per serving

*P*OACHED PEARS WITH APRICOTS

PREPARATION TIME: 8 minutes
COOKING TIME: 10 minutes

Serve these pears piping hot with ice cream melting over them.

SERVES 4

25 g (1 oz) butter or margarine
25 g (1 oz) soft brown sugar
15 ml (1 tbsp) lemon juice
700 g (1½ lb) ripe but firm pears
50 g (2 oz) no-soak dried apricots
15 ml (1 tbsp) Grand Marnier or brandy
chopped nuts, to decorate
ice cream or fresh cream, to serve

1 Put the butter, sugar and lemon juice in a saucepan with 150 ml (¼ pint) water and warm together.
2 Peel, quarter and core the pears. Halve each quarter again if large. Snip the apricots into shreds.
3 Add the pears and apricots to the syrup, cover and simmer for 5–10 minutes or until the pears are just tender. Stir in the Grand Marnier.
4 Serve hot, sprinkled with chopped nuts and topped with ice cream or fresh cream.

NOT SUITABLE FOR FREEZING

195 Calories per serving

Overleaf: Left to right: Poached Pears with Apricots; Walnut and Orange Puddings; Prune and Nut Crumble

Mulled Summer Fruits

PREPARATION TIME: 5 minutes
COOKING TIME: 5 minutes

SERVES 4

450 g (1 lb) summer fruits, such as strawberries, cherries, raspberries, redcurrants, etc.
300 ml (½ pint) apple juice
25 g (1 oz) caster sugar
pared rind of ½ lemon
2 cloves
1 cinnamon stick
pinch of ground mixed spice
double cream and chopped fresh mint, to serve

1 Carefully pick over the fruit, hull and prepare as necessary. Place in a large bowl.
2 Gently heat the apple juice and sugar together until the sugar dissolves. Add the remaining ingredients and bring to the boil, stirring.
3 Remove from the heat and leave to stand for 2 minutes before straining over the fruit. Serve immediately with cream flavoured with mint.

NOT SUITABLE FOR FREEZING

80 Calories per serving

Fall Fruit Salad

PREPARATION TIME: 20 minutes
COOKING TIME: nil

You may think it unusual to serve a fresh fruit salad with a vinaigrette dressing, but the sharpness of the vinegar intensifies the flavours of the fruit. You'll find balsamic vinegar, a rich, sweet-sour vinegar from Italy, in delicatessens and supermarkets.

SERVES 8

3 pomegranates
7.5 ml (1½ tsp) balsamic vinegar
10 ml (2 tsp) olive oil
10 ml (2 tsp) walnut oil
salt and pepper
125 g (4 oz) large seedless green grapes
125 g (4 oz) seedless black grapes
8 ripe figs
2 oranges
3 prickly pears (optional)
175 g (6 oz) Comice pears
175 g (6 oz) red eating apples

1 Halve the pomegranates and scoop out the seeds. Place about two-thirds in a food processor and purée to extract the juice, then strain into a jug. Whisk in the vinegar, oils and seasoning.
2 Halve the grapes. Thinly slice the figs. Peel the oranges of all skin and pith, and thinly slice the fruit. Peel and slice the prickly pears, if using. (Remember to wear rubber gloves when handling prickly pears, to avoid hurting your hands on the sharp spines.) Halve, core and thinly slice the pears and apples.
3 Mix the prepared fruits and divide between six flat plates. Spoon a little vinaigrette over the fruits and serve.

NOT SUITABLE FOR FREEZING

160 Calories per serving

*H*OT PINEAPPLE AND BANANA SALAD

PREPARATION TIME: 15 minutes
COOKING TIME: 12 minutes

You will find creamed coconut on sale in most super-markets, usually beside the spices. Any you don't use will keep well in the fridge for up to 3 months.

SERVES 4

1 small pineapple, about 900 g (2 lb)
4 small bananas, about 450 g (1 lb) total weight
25 g (1 oz) butter or margarine
soft brown sugar
30 ml (2 tbsp) Malibu, rum or orange juice
FOR THE COCONUT SAUCE (OPTIONAL)
50 g (2 oz) creamed coconut
75 ml (3 fl oz) boiling water
sugar

1 Peel and slice the pineapple, then peel and thickly slice the bananas.
2 Melt the butter or margarine in a large sauté pan, add 5 ml (1 level tsp) sugar and heat for 1 minute. Add the pineapple and sauté gently for 3–4 minutes, until beginning to soften and brown. Add the banana and sauté for a further 3 minutes. Pour in the Malibu, rum or orange juice.
3 To make the coconut sauce, if using, place the creamed coconut and water in a small saucepan. Stir until smooth. Add a pinch of sugar to taste, then gently bring to the boil. Simmer for 1 minute and serve with the fruit.

NOT SUITABLE FOR FREEZING

173 Calories per serving without sauce
261 Calories per serving with sauce

*S*UGARED BLACKBERRY AND APPLE PANCAKES

PREPARATION TIME: 5 minutes
COOKING TIME: 10 minutes

Ready-made pancakes can be found in many super-markets – they are great timesavers. Keep some stored in the freezer for up to 2 months.

SERVES 4

350 g (12 oz) jar or can chunky apple, unsweetened
225 g (8 oz) fresh blackberries
2.5 ml (½ level tsp) ground mixed spice
4 large or 8 small ready-made pancakes
butter
lemon juice
icing sugar
25 g (1 oz) toasted flaked almonds
soured cream, to serve (optional)

1 Mix together the apple, blackberries and mixed spice.
2 Halve large pancakes; if using small ones, leave them whole. Roll into cornet shapes and fill with the blackberry and apple mixture. Place the cornets, seam-side down, in a lightly buttered, ovenproof dish.
3 Dot the pancakes with butter and sprinkle with lemon juice. Cover loosely with foil.
4 Bake in the oven at 200°C (400°F) mark 6 for 10 minutes. Dust generously with icing sugar and scatter over the flaked almonds. Serve with soured cream, if wished.

NOT SUITABLE FOR FREEZING

450 Calories per serving

Overleaf: Left to right: Filo-Topped Apple Pie (page 123); Pears with Ginger Cheese (page 123); Figs with Warm Berry Sauce (page 122)

*P*EARS IN FILO

PREPARATION TIME: 10 minutes
COOKING TIME: 20–25 minutes

SERVES 4

75 g (3 oz) no-soak pitted prunes, roughly chopped
25 g (1 oz) pecan nuts or walnuts, roughly chopped
15 ml (1 level tbsp) demerara sugar
pinch of ground cinnamon
30 ml (2 tbsp) unsweetened apple or orange juice
grated rind and juice of ½ lemon
4 ripe pears, preferably Williams, about 550 g (1¼ lb) total weight
4 sheets of filo pastry, each about 28 cm (11 inches) square
25 g (1 oz) butter, melted
fromage frais, to serve

1 Mix the prunes and nuts together with the sugar, cinnamon, apple or orange juice and grated rind and juice of the lemon.
2 Peel the pears, cut off the stalks and remove the cores with an apple corer, leaving the pears whole.
3 Place each pear in the centre of a piece of filo pastry, then fill the centre of the pear with the prune mixture. Wrap the pastry around each pear to enclose completely. Pinch the top of the pastry to form a purse. Lightly brush with melted butter.
4 Bake in the oven at 190°C (375°F) mark 5 for 20–25 minutes or until crisp, golden brown and cooked through, covering loosely with foil if necessary. Serve immediately, accompanied by the fromage frais.

NOT SUITABLE FOR FREEZING

245 Calories per serving

*F*IGS WITH WARM BERRY SAUCE

PREPARATION TIME: 5 minutes
COOKING TIME: 3 minutes

SERVES 4

8 ripe figs
215 g (7½ oz) can blackberries in apple juice
10 ml (2 level tsp) icing sugar
5 ml (1 level tsp) arrowroot
mint or lemon geranium leaves or borage flowers, to decorate (optional)

1 Cut the stalks off the figs. In each fig, make two cuts in a cross shape, from the stalk end, three-quarters of the way through. Open up to resemble flowers, and place two figs on each of four serving plates.
2 Push the blackberries and juice through a nylon sieve into a small saucepan. Add the icing sugar. Mix the arrowroot to a smooth paste with a little water.
3 Gently heat the blackberry sauce until simmering, then remove from the heat and stir in the arrowroot. Return to the heat and boil for 1 minute.
4 Pour a little sauce over each fig. Decorate with mint or lemon geranium leaves or borage flowers, if wished. Serve the remaining sauce in a separate jug.

NOT SUITABLE FOR FREEZING

70 Calories per serving

VARIATION

Try serving this simple berry sauce with slices of Galia melon or quartered fresh pears.

*P*EARS WITH GINGER CHEESE

PREPARATION TIME: 10 minutes
COOKING TIME: nil

SERVES 4

415 g (14½ oz) can pear halves in fruit juice
225 g (8 oz) natural cottage cheese
grated rind of 1 lemon
icing sugar
15 g (½ oz) stem ginger, finely chopped
15 g (½ oz) pistachio nuts, finely chopped

1 Drain the juice from the pear halves and dry them on absorbent kitchen paper. Slice thinly and arrange on four serving plates.
2 Sieve the cottage cheese into a bowl and fold in the lemon rind, 5 ml (1 level tsp) icing sugar and the ginger.
3 Serve the pears accompanied by the ginger cheese, decorated with nuts and dusted with icing sugar.

NOT SUITABLE FOR FREEZING

160 Calories per serving

VARIATION

Fromage frais could replace the cottage cheese, in which case there's no need to sieve it.

*F*ILO-TOPPED APPLE PIE

PREPARATION TIME: 10 minutes
COOKING TIME: 15 minutes

SERVES 4

383 g (13½ oz) can apple slices
2.5 ml (½ level tsp) ground mixed spice
2.5 ml (½ level tsp) ground cinnamon
sugar
25 g (1 oz) sultanas
1 sheet of filo pastry, 45.5×28 cm (18×11 inches)
15 g (½ oz) butter, melted

1 Drain the apples, reserving the juice. In a bowl, mix together the spices, sugar, sultanas and apple slices with about 30 ml (2 tbsp) juice. Mix well and spoon into a small, shallow oven-proof dish.
2 Brush one side of the pastry with melted butter, then tear it into pieces and arrange over the pie, with the buttered side up.
3 Bake in the oven at 220°C (425°F) mark 7 for about 15 minutes or until golden brown. Serve warm.

NOT SUITABLE FOR FREEZING

147 Calories per serving

Raspberry Yogurt Fool

PREPARATION TIME: 5 minutes
COOKING TIME: 2 minutes

SERVES 4

385 g (13½ oz) can raspberries in syrup
15 ml (1 level tbsp) arrowroot
30 ml (2 tbsp) runny honey
450 g (1 lb) Greek-style yogurt
mint sprigs, to decorate
shortbread or coconut fingers, to serve

1 Drain the raspberries in a nylon sieve and reserve the syrup. Blend the arrowroot with 15 ml (1 tbsp) of the syrup, then stir into the remainder. Bring to the boil, stirring, and cook for 1 minute. Add the raspberries, then leave to cool.
2 Mix the honey with the yogurt and spoon alternate layers of the cold raspberries and yogurt into four dishes. Swirl together, using a skewer. Decorate with mint sprigs and serve with sweet biscuits.

NOT SUITABLE FOR FREEZING

235 Calories per serving

❧

Apricot Orange Crisp

PREPARATION TIME: 10 minutes
COOKING TIME: 10 minutes

SERVES 4

grated rind and juice of ½ small orange
two 397 g (14 oz) cans apricot halves in natural juice, drained

75 g (3 oz) butter or margarine
175 g (6 oz) plain flour
50 g (2 oz) chopped blanched almonds
50 g (2 oz) demerara sugar
single cream, Greek-style yogurt or custard, to serve

1 Stir the orange rind and juice into the fruit and warm in a saucepan. Spoon into a 1.1 litre (2 pint) flameproof dish.
2 While the fruit is warming, rub the fat into the flour until the mixture resembles breadcrumbs. Stir in the almonds and sugar, then sprinkle over the apricots and grill lightly. Serve warm with cream, yogurt or custard.

SUITABLE FOR FREEZING

430 Calories per serving

❧

Tropical Fruit Dessert with Orange Liqueur

PREPARATION TIME: 5 minutes
COOKING TIME: 5 minutes

SERVES 6

two 410 g (14½ oz) cans tropical fruit cocktail in pineapple and passionfruit juice
2 passionfruit
30 ml (2 tbsp) orange-flavoured liqueur
4 medium scoops vanilla ice cream
mint sprigs, to decorate

1 Drain the fruit cocktail, reserving the juice of one can only. Halve the passionfruit, scoop out the pulp and seeds, and reserve.
2 Place the reserved fruit juice in a small saucepan and boil until reduced by half. Stir in

the liqueur and the passionfruit pulp and seeds. Pour the warm juice over the fruit.

3 Serve immediately, accompanied by vanilla ice cream and decorated with mint sprigs.

NOT SUITABLE FOR FREEZING

125 Calories per serving

Cinnamon Apple Slices

PREPARATION TIME: 10 minutes
COOKING TIME: 15 minutes

SERVES 4

50–75 g (2–3 oz) butter
4 small currant buns, split in half
2 eating apples, peeled, cored and cut into rings
45 ml (3 level tbsp) demerara sugar
1.25 ml (¼ level tsp) ground cinnamon
icing sugar, to dust
Greek-style yogurt, to serve

1 Butter the buns thickly on both sides and place on a baking sheet. Top each half with three halved apple rings and sprinkle with the demerara sugar and cinnamon.

2 Bake in the oven at 200°C (400°F) mark 6 for 15 minutes or until the apples are golden brown and cooked through. Dust with icing sugar and serve with Greek yogurt.

NOT SUITABLE FOR FREEZING

280 Calories per serving

VARIATION

Peel, core and slice two pears and use in place of the apple.

Spiced Fruit Brûlée

PREPARATION TIME: 10 minutes
COOKING TIME: 15 minutes

Any mixture of dried fruit could be used to make this wonderfully spicy seasonal pudding.

SERVES 4

175 g (6 oz) dried apple rings
50 g (2 oz) no-soak pitted prunes
50 g (2 oz) no-soak dried apricots
600 ml (1 pint) water
pared rind and juice of 1 orange
pared rind and juice of 1 lemon
pinch of ground cloves and freshly grated nutmeg
1 cinnamon stick
142 ml (5 fl oz) carton natural yogurt
30 ml (2 tbsp) runny honey
10 ml (2 level tsp) demerara sugar

1 Place the dried fruit in a saucepan with the water, the pared orange and lemon rind, the juice of the orange and 15 ml (1 tbsp) lemon juice. Add the ground cloves and nutmeg and the cinnamon stick. Bring to the boil and simmer gently for about 10 minutes, or until the fruit is tender but do not allow it to turn mushy.

2 Meanwhile, mix together the yogurt and honey until smooth and blended.

3 Drain the fruit, reserving the juices, and arrange on four flameproof serving plates. Pour over a little of the juices. Spoon the yogurt on top and sprinkle a little of the demerara sugar over each plate.

4 Place each plate under a preheated grill until the topping is bubbling and golden brown. Serve immediately.

NOT SUITABLE FOR FREEZING

160 Calories per serving

CHOCOLATE MUFFINS

PREPARATION TIME: 10–15 minutes
COOKING TIME: 20 minutes

SERVES 6

65 g (2½ oz) self-raising flour
1.25 ml (¼ level tsp) baking powder
small pinch of salt
75 ml (5 level tbsp) drinking chocolate powder
15 ml (1 tbsp) vegetable oil
2.5 ml (½ tsp) vanilla essence
1 egg, beaten
25 ml (1 fl oz) skimmed milk
25 g (1 oz) plain chocolate, roughly chopped
15 g (½ oz) walnut pieces, roughly chopped
10 ml (2 level tsp) arrowroot
300 ml (½ pint) cold water

1 Sift the flour and baking powder into a bowl, then add the salt and 30 ml (2 level tbsp) chocolate powder.
2 Make a well in the centre and add the oil, vanilla essence, egg and milk. Beat well until smooth, then gently stir in the chocolate and walnuts.
3 Place six individual paper cake cases on a baking sheet. Spoon the mixture into the cases – it should be about 0.5 cm (¼ inch) from the top of each one. Bake in the oven at 220°C (425°F) mark 7 for 15 minutes or until firm to the touch and well risen.
4 To make the chocolate sauce, place the remaining chocolate powder in a small saucepan with the arrowroot. Stir in 100 ml (4 fl oz) water to form a smooth paste. Add the remaining water.
5 Slowly bring to the boil and cook for 30 seconds only, stirring all the time. Turn out the muffins and serve hot with the chocolate sauce.

NOT SUITABLE FOR FREEZING

160 Calories per serving

VARIATION

Omit the chocolate and walnuts, and replace with one roughly chopped banana.

INDEX